The Preacher's Library

Preaching as Doctrine

'to be a window, through thy grace'

John B Taylor

Other titles in the series

1 *Why Preach?*, Peter Dawson
2 *Preaching on the Old Testament*, Christine Pilkington
3 *Variety in Preaching*, Brian Galliers
4 *Preaching in a Cultural Context*, Martyn D Atkins
5 *A Woman's Perspective on Preaching*, Jane V Craske

ISBN 1 85852 194 7

For John Rogan, who got me into the story

The Reverend Dr John B Taylor is currently the Chair of the Liverpool District of the Methodist Church. In addition to his circuit experience as a minister, he has been University Chaplain in Sheffield, Tutor in Systematic Theology at the Queen's College in Birmingham and General Secretary of the Division of Ministries, with especial responsibility for Initial Ministerial Training. He is a former Convener of the Faith & Order Committee and in 1997-1998 was President of the Methodist Conference.

GENERAL INTRODUCTION

Preaching is a very particular form of communication which has always been important in the life of the Christian Church. At the beginning of the 21st century we are undergoing a revolution in the varieties, method and speed of our communications. Preachers of all denominations, ordained and lay, undertake this calling with an awareness that we preach in a changing context.

The Preacher's Library is designed to help us to think through, perhaps in some cases reassess, why we preach, how we preach, and to whom we preach. Some of the volumes in this series will take a fresh look at familiar issues, such as how preachers should approach various parts of the Bible, how we understand and express our doctrinal inheritance and the variety of styles in which preaching can be done. Other volumes will introduce issues which may be less familiar to many of us, such as the significance of our cultural context or the way in which the self-understanding of a woman preacher has important things to say to all preachers. Some of these books will offer direct help in the practice of preaching. Others will deal with issues which, although they appear more theoretical, impinge upon the preacher's task and on which we therefore need to have reflected if we are to preach with integrity in today's world.

All the writers in this series, lay and ordained, women and men, are recognised preachers within their own denominations and write with the needs of their colleagues firmly in mind. These books will avoid academic jargon, but they will not avoid dealing with difficult issues. They are offered to other preachers in the belief that as we deepen our thinking and hone our skills

God's people will be blessed and built up to the glory of God.

Some of us are hesitant about preaching on doctrinal themes because such preaching is identified in many people's minds with boring, dry and overly academic sermons. Sadly, that has often been the case, but in this stimulating and imaginative book John Taylor shows that it does not need to be. Our understanding of God – and therefore theology and doctrine – is shaped by the story of Jesus. The first disciples felt themselves, in Dr Taylor's words, 'pushed by their experience to conclusions that no one would have wanted to invent'. To preach about Christian doctrine is therefore essentially about how we tell that story today and how we draw out its implications for contemporary discipleship. If we learn well from what John Taylor writes our congregations will hear sermons which deepen and strengthen faith even as they also connect with lived Christian experience.

Michael J Townsend

CONTENTS

FOREWORD

Lord, how can man preach thy eternall word?
He is a brittle crazie glass:
Yet in thy temple thou dost him afford
This glorious and transcendent place,
To be a window, through thy grace.[1]

It has always seemed to me to be a wonderful privilege as well as an awesome responsibility to be called to be a preacher. My vestry prayer has therefore been over the years: 'O Lord, speak through me and help me not to get in the way.' The problem is '. . . preaching is the bringing of truth through personality',[2] as preachers have been used to being told for well over a hundred years. Indeed, how could it not be so? No one has seen God at any time. The message is always a refracted one. A preacher should therefore approach the designated task humbly, in fear and trembling, asking 'to be a window, through thy grace'.

There are four movements to the argument of this book. Chapter 1 is intended to open up some theological issues facing the preacher and looks at the sources of our knowledge of God. Having determined that the preacher's chief medium of communication is story, chapter 2 examines the nature of story and shows how it functions. Chapter 3 is an attempt to get inside the story of Jesus to try and see what it must have been like for the first disciples living with him day by day. The challenge is to identify the issues they faced and to try and understand why they reacted as they did. We travel with them from the lakeside to the cross. Chapter 4 tries to take hold of the major areas of reflection which were imposed on the early Church by the belief that the crucifixion was not the end. The hinge on which everything Christian depends is the resurrection. Ascension, Pentecost, Trinity, Advent,

Christmas, the mystery of creation and our redemption, all have to be discussed in the light of the belief that Christ is alive.

Walking first with the disciples and then reflecting on their experience of Christ is not always an easy division to make. Even those parts of the Scriptures which seem to be fairly straightforward narrative are in fact overlaid in many subtle ways with interpretation of their meaning. However, basic to the whole enterprise is the belief that the developed doctrine of the Church has to be reappropriated in every generation. The task of preachers is to offer to their hearers a story into which they are invited in order to experience truth for themselves.

In what follows I acknowledge my debt to many, many people who have shaped me over the years. Wherever possible I have acknowledged that debt. However, in the course of time some things become so much a part of us that we are no longer aware where they came from. If I have failed to remember, please forgive me.

I am particularly indebted to Mrs Florence Martin for her hard work in helping me to type the manuscript and in tracking down pieces of information, all of which has saved me hours and ultimately made the appearance of this material possible.

John B Taylor

1

FEAR OF THEOLOGY

The former Prime Minister, Harold Wilson, Lord Wilson of Rievaulx, is rightly held in high esteem. None the less he is often brought out as an aunt Sally to shy at because of his use of the word 'theology'. In his famous speech on Clause 4 of the Labour Party Constitution, famous at the very least amongst theologians, Lord Wilson dismissed the elements of the constitution which were not related to the daily business of political life as 'the theology of it all', clearly understanding theology to be something that can safely be ignored as irrelevant for normal everyday working. The best theology, however, arises out of real life situations and has practical consequences for the way people live. Nevertheless, Lord Wilson's understanding of the word theology is one widely shared, not only by people outside the faith communities but also by many believers. It is not uncommon to hear a cry for the 'simple' gospel – whatever that is. Doctrine and dogma are spoken of scathingly, as if they were perversely invented to bamboozle ordinary folk, whereas those in training for ministry within the life of the Church are constantly urged to think theologically. Theological reflection is the watchword of the day.

There can, of course, be little dispute that much specialised learning separates those in ministry from the people to whom they minister, as the language of the doctor, indeed any specialist, can create an impression of great learning and little else. It certainly does not communicate with most people. My dear old father-in-law who lived with us after the death of his wife would often go to the chapel of the Theological College where I taught at the time. When he came back he would say: 'By, that preacher must've been clever. I didn't understand a word that was said.' Such comments are heard not just in Theological College chapels but in congregations throughout these islands. There are clearly preachers and teachers who are more concerned with impressing folk with their great learning than with communicating anything at all, never mind the 'simple gospel'. True learning coming from the truly learned will be expressed in such a way that the hearers will wonder why they never thought of it in that way before.

So, let us translate some of the expressions which belong to today's community of faith. What is theology?[3] It is talking and thinking about God. To reflect theologically is to ask of the situation in which we find ourselves: 'What, if anything, has God got to do with this? What has this got to do with God?' For example: to think theologically about, say, wealth creation is to ask precisely what, if anything, has God got to do with making money? And we need people to ask such questions. Not just the ordained, with their assumed special knowledge, which can distance them from the hurly-burly of the world, but also a theologically literate laity, men and women, who are far more likely to have to deal with the hard questions that rarely, if ever, get across the church steps. To think theologically is something which the whole people of God needs to learn, not least the lay and ordained people who occupy our pulpits, if what they say is to have anything to do with the lives of the population at large. However, if we are to think theologically there are some questions which have to be asked by way of preamble.

What is God like?

It would be a matter of considerable concern if God were 'a one-eyed yellow idol to the north of Khatmandu', who in J Milton Hayes' dramatic monologue wreaks revenge on Mad Carew for the theft of 'the little green eye of the god'. We would probably spend our time seeking ways of keeping this kind of god sweet. Fortunately, Christians do not believe that the God known through Jesus is a vindictive idol who has to be placated. He is, they believe, a God of love who wants us to enter into a free, loving relationship with him.

Johnston R McKay, in the course of the Mair Lectures in the University of Glasgow in 1995, quotes the words of two people he says that he covets for Christianity:[4]

> The first from a conversation I once had with a very wise, but very blunt man. 'You preachers have got it all wrong,' he told me. 'You seem to be saying that Jesus was son of God and that's why we should follow him; but maybe you should be asking us to follow him and leaving us to discover that he was the son of God.'
>
> The second signal comes from that incomparable religious journalist, the late Gerald Priestland. 'One morning,' he said, 'as I was coming home from my daily contemplative stroll, I found myself saying: 'If Jesus was not the son of God, he is now.' I cannot believe that Jesus intended his followers to say, 'You are the second person of the Trinity'. . . What I do believe is that the company of his followers has come to see God almost exclusively through him; has come to say, 'God is like this.' God is so like this that as far as we can ever tell, God is this. For we are not likely to come any closer.

The fact of the matter is that Christians believe that the principal way of understanding what God is like is to look at Jesus of Nazareth whose disciples came to believe as they followed him that he is indeed the Messiah, the Son of the living God and the Second Person of the

Trinity. In Christian terms, if you want to know what God is like, you must look to Jesus. However, to make the discovery that Jesus is, in fact, our best clue to understanding the nature and being of God we have to *do* theology, participate in the community of faith, rather than merely study it.

It is clearly possible to try to understand God in Jewish terms or Muslim terms. It is possible to try and see God as a Hindu or a Sikh might do it. It would be Christian arrogance to claim that adherents of other faiths can know nothing of God or simply to dismiss them all as idolators. Many people *do,* however, manage to talk about God, to study theology even from a Christian perspective by walking around it as if it were a porcelain vase on a stand, to be described dispassionately. But the first step to *doing* theology is to do what the first disciples of Jesus did. We have to step within the circle of faith and obey when he says to us: 'Come, follow me', (see below chapter 3), where following is a lifelong activity, for there is always more to learn about the nature and being of God. There can never be a point where we have it all sewn up, even when we have reached the point in the Christian narrative where we say with Thomas: 'My Lord and my God!' I became a Christian at the age of 15. I'll tell the story in a later part of this book but I remain a Christian 50 years on because the service of the God and Father of our Lord Jesus Christ still makes the best sense I know of the world around me. It provides coherence and a more than adequate basis for daily living. It has been a journey of constant discovery and surprise. I shall stick with it whilst it makes sufficient sense and whilst it says as a minimum what needs to be said. At the end of the day, though, as Fred Craddock puts it:

> The real question is, In what kind of God do we believe? Does the God in whom we believe fuel a life of cruelty and privilege and exclusion or does that God call us to kindness, to justice, and to inclusion? Now enter Jesus Christ. The God in whom we believe is the

> God revealed in the ministry, death, and resurrection of Jesus . . .[5]

It matters who God is. It makes a difference to our theological reflection whether God is capricious and whimsical and likely to stroke us at one minute and swat us at the next, or whether he is indeed the God and Father of our Lord Jesus Christ, a God of love and beauty who is faithful to his children and intends them to grow and flourish and thrive and prosper. It makes a world of difference to the way we look and where we look for signs of his activity in the world.

How do we know anything about him?

There is a real problem in trying to talk about God at all, if theology is not to be a projection of human beings, humanity writ large. *If* God is, as most people *suppose,* the Creator and Sustainer of all that is, beyond our finite human knowledge, eternal, all-wise, 'in light inaccessible, hid from our eyes' and so on, then human beings can only know anything at all about God if God is prepared to reveal his being to them. I have put the word *if* in italics and the word *suppose* in italics because no one can either affirm God's existence or deny it from a position free of presuppositions and assumptions. The important thing is to be as aware as we can be of the nature of the assumptions we make. I am operating with the assumption that *if* there is a God, we can only know something about him *if* he does make himself known. He is beyond my imagining. However, if God's self-revelation is the primary assumption I make to make God-talk possible, even our assumptions about God will not go unchallenged. I am very conscious as I write that for many people the use of the male pronoun, for example, speaking of God as 'he' is an assumption too far. God, if he really is God, must be beyond gender, even if the use of the male pronoun does belong to the patriarchal tradition of which I am a part.

Another presupposition with which many people live is that God is all-powerful. 'Almighty God . . .' is the beginning of many a Christian prayer. If God's omnipotence is the ability to do anything, that 'given' is challenged by the weak and vulnerable Christ on the cross – again if the one God is to be known through Jesus of Nazareth. At the very least we would have to say that God did not use his power to rescue Jesus, that God must have had some other purpose, some other end in view, in not intervening.

Now, if knowledge of God can only be gained because God has chosen to reveal himself to humanity, where do we look to receive this self-revelation? Some would say that something of God's nature and being can be read off from the world around us in much the same way as we can learn something about painters by looking at the canvases they produce. Even then it would be my contention that such knowledge is only possible if God reveals himself first. However, it is the faith of Christians and the presumption underlying the doing of theology that God's supreme revelation of himself has taken place through the life, death and resurrection of Jesus whose first disciples recognised him as the Christ. He is the prism through whom our knowledge of God is refracted. For Christians he is the yardstick by which we measure the truth or falsehood of what we believe and say about God. This, however, cannot just be asserted. '. . . revelation is something that happens, not something that is reported.'[6] It is something which happens to us. We cannot organise it. So, because it comes from God Christians have often a strong sense of being 'chosen', as indeed the people of Israel felt chosen by God to be a light to the rest of the world.

The Scriptures

In asking where we turn for knowledge of the God made known through Jesus we rapidly become conscious of a whole cluster of ideas which gather around the notion of 'scripture'. The books of the Bible are often called collectively the word of God. They are spoken of as 'inspired', some claiming that they are 'inerrant', that is that they have been protected by the Holy Spirit from the possibility of error. Some accord little or no role to the human authors, regarding them as little more than instruments chosen to record God's word. Some give to the human authors a much larger part in the production of the books that bear their names. Many have been keen to assert that the Scriptures contain all we need to know for our salvation.

So, what is meant by saying that the books of the Bible are inspired and by calling them the word of God? 'All scripture is inspired by God' (2 Timothy 3:16), we are told. In context that saying must refer to the Hebrew Scriptures of the Old Testament, although in the history of the Church the idea of inspiration was also early applied to some of the books of our New Testament. Even within the New Testament corpus, as is clearly the case in 2 Peter, some of the epistles of Paul have become scripture in the developing Christian canon. Certainly it is common practice in the context of worship to refer to the Bible as the word of God. Is there something objective, the words of the Bible themselves, which can be called the word of God? Or do the words only become the word of God when actually apprehended as such? John Dillenberger in *The New Hermeneutic* is surely right when he says that the word of God is the bringing of the text that was once proclamation into fresh proclamation, that is, into the situation where it again becomes faith.

Furthermore, the Church of England Report *Christian Believing* contains these very significant sentences:

> To speak of the Bible as 'the word of God' or 'the Word of God in the words of men [sic]', is just as much a judgement of faith as to speak of some historical event as 'an act of God'. It is not a proposition that can be proved.[7]

The Bible on my bookshelf is not the word of God as it stands there and it does no good to hit people over the head with the solemn pronouncement that this is the word of God, if they do not already share the presupposition that the Bible possesses an authority which demands to be heard. It only becomes the word of God when we are addressed by what it says and grasped by a sense of truth which cannot be gainsaid.

This is what might be called a poetic model of inspiration. Inspiration takes place when we are grasped by a vision, a thought or idea, which seems to us self-evidently true. We may be actively searching for something or we may be taken unawares but a new apprehension of truth invades us. It is experienced not just as a good idea that we have dreamt up but as a new insight, something 'given' which opens up new vistas and changes our perspectives. For the Christian inspiration may be experienced in dialogue with the Scriptures which are the deposit of Christian faith, the record of responses to the God who is made known through Jesus Christ.

In this respect poetry and religion are linguistically similar. They both speak on the 'edges of language' as Paul van Buren says. They stretch language beyond its everyday limits. They create the opportunity for new insights. In this sense poets and other writers often feel that an idea or a vision has taken them over. They have been grasped by something beyond themselves. They have become the servant of the vision. In a similar way those who are attentive to their text will be grasped by the vision they have received, if they have expressed it clearly and have not themselves got in the way of it. The vision offered may impose itself upon the readers of the text or the hearers of the words because it authentically expresses the truth about the world they know and takes them beyond it. One of the reasons why Christians constantly return to a text they have read and heard many times is because everyone comes to it carrying their own personal baggage. It is not possible to come uncluttered. Each comes as black or white, male or female, young or old, with his or her own emotional, spiritual and intellectual apparatus, bringing inbred cultural assumptions. In the technical jargon the art of interpreting ancient texts is called 'hermeneutics' and the effect of constantly changing in our contact with those texts is called the 'hermeneutical spiral'. Each time we read the Scriptures we risk being given new insight and changed so that that new position becomes the starting-point of our next encounter.

In this way of approaching the Scriptures, the writers felt that they had been grasped by the vision. They were somehow given an understanding, a burden, a word from beyond themselves. The origin of truth is outside of them. They were inspired and those who read, hear and study the Scriptures may also be grasped by fresh insights into the nature and being of God. If it is true, as I have claimed, that human beings can only know something about God if God chooses to reveal himself, in this sense the writers of the books of the Bible feel that they have been given a vision which it is their task to communicate. They have been given a message which is not their own but comes from God.

The biblical books as a whole are literature and can be read as such, as the record of the faith of people long ago. Christians, however, are incapable of reading them as mere literature. They accord to this collection of books a special status because it is *believed* (a faith statement) that their principal subject matter is the relationship between God and human beings and between human beings and God. They are a treasury of the ways in which those relationships have been lived out over hundreds of years. They are not the free creation of the human imagination but claim that they are anchored in real historical events. In particular, they bear witness to one man whom they believe to be the Word of God made flesh. Furthermore, they are read publicly in a formal liturgical setting and over the centuries have been experienced as mediating a message from God. It is this experience which makes them a yardstick of Christian worship and practice. In these combined respects the Bible is unique and different from any other writing.

If the Scriptures are unique in this way, it is difficult to see them as dictated from on high, as if God used the writers to do some automatic writing. The word of God, using a poetic model of inspiration, is a mediated word, refracted through people and therefore inevitably historically conditioned and in need of constant interpretation. The authors may express their vision imperfectly. Furthermore, if indeed the Scriptures contain centuries of testimony to people's vision of and relationship with God, the very variety of response to God is immensely liberating. I find it helpful to think of Pythagoras' theorem. In a right-angled triangle the square on the hypotenuse is equal to the sum of the squares on the other two sides. As long as we are talking of a right-angled triangle it will always be true. There can, however, be an infinite number of worked examples. It all depends on the size of the right-angled triangle. Similarly the New Testament Scriptures call upon us to make our response to the claim that God loves us.

In the gospels we have stories about how the first disciples made their corporate and individual response to the love of God. The beauty is that the response of Simon Peter was different from the reponse of James and John. They all responded in their own way to the love of God made known in Jesus, a fact which we each in our individual uniqueness ought to find liberating. We are free to make our own response without having to imitate any other Christian, however ancient and however venerable. There is room for every person to respond to the theorem that God loves us.

So, the authority of the Scriptures is, I believe, best conceived as residing in the fact that the Scriptures are the deposit of God's dealings with people in history. They are authoritative in a way no other book could be because of their closeness to the focal point of Christian belief, the presence and activity of God revealed to us through the life and ministry of Jesus of Nazareth. We accord authority to the Old Testament over the shape of our lives because the Hebrew Scriptures were the cradle in which Jesus was born. His self-understanding and his vision of God were shaped against the background of what Christians call the Old Testament. The New Testament gives an over-the-shoulder account of him with the benefit of the marvellous gift of hindsight, and it is the permanent standard witness to Jesus. It has been found in the course of history since the time of Jesus to constitute a reliable guide for understanding what human life is about, that is to say that the New Testament writings have been heard over the years as offering a credible vision of God and his world, speaking to women and men a word from God.

Although the canon of the New Testament was more or less fixed by the fourth century of the Christian era, the books included were never a dead deposit. It was believed, and is believed, that the letter of the writings is continually kept alive by the activity of God himself through the work of the Holy Spirit. Through the record of many people's responses the texts still mediate God's presence and activity today. Christian doctrine is not a changeless body of truth, drawn up once for all. Its transmission is not like handing on the family treasure, but we do have to find a way of bridging the two thousand years between us and the period which the texts describe. This is partly done by exegesis, trying to discover what the texts meant for the people who wrote and read two millennia ago. But that is not enough.

> As we study the writings of the past the question we have always to be asking is: what must the truth have been and be if men [sic] who thought and spoke as they did saw it and spoke of it like that.[8]

Leonard Hodgson's famous question has stood the test of time. It helps us to appreciate that the New Testament is not a static text set in stone.

> Rather it is a matter of a series of responses to the divine acts in Christ, responses which always have an experimental nature. They are always an attempt to solve a specific problem; how in the light of these circumstances, thinking as we do in the world we live in, do

> the data appear, and what response do they demand of us.[9]

The test of good Christian doctrine lies in its appropriateness as response, not just in the past but also today. It also means that no response is the definitive word. The terms of the experiment change. So, the Bible only becomes the word of God when reader-listeners become aware that what people responded to long ago is also addressed to them. When people find themselves grasped by truth from beyond and when they respond by committing themselves, the words they have been reading become for them the word of God. In the end we are confronted in the New Testament by a person, Jesus of Nazareth, whom the Church has held up to the world as the supreme revelation of what God is like. The Scriptures give sufficient knowledge of what is necessary for our salvation (cf. The 39 Articles, Article 6). They provide the ground rules for the ongoing dialogue between the living God and the living, worshipping community of which the individual is a part. In that story the figure of Jesus is the central, focal point.

The tradition of the Church

As well as the Scriptures, a second major witness, of a different kind, is the Church. The text of scripture is permanent and unchanging. The Church, an historical institution, is changing and changeable. Of course, the traditions of the Church are in one respect prior to the writing of the books of the New Testament. It was a group of disciples who first told stories about Jesus and invited reflection on their meaning before anything was written down. The gospels are not a statement of bare fact. Interpretation of the events surrounding Jesus is interwoven with biographical material which itself is not all of the same kind. However, the initial impetus to the rise of the Church came from the telling of the stories about the life and ministry of Jesus by the first apostles. It could never be detached testimony for they had lived with him and were themselves involved in the story. They themselves were right from the beginning wrestling with the significance of what they had experienced. When in his speech on the day of Pentecost Peter speaks of Jesus as the fulfilment of prophecy the process of reflection is under way.

The clear benefit of taking the Church seriously as a witness to what God has done in Jesus the Christ is that, after the production of the fixed record in scripture, its testimony is a flesh and blood witness in the present, in real people. The disadvantage is that the testimony of the Church gets further and further removed in time from Jesus Christ and the focal events surrounding him. There is undoubtedly room for error in its witness. The accuracy of what it proclaims is more open to question. Yet I believe that the tradition of the Church must be taken seriously as a 2000 year long testimony concerning what God has done and will yet do amongst us. It is, however, important that we look at the Church in the context of our basic knowledge of God.

The Church is a body of people characterised by certain activities and attitudes of which theology is one, but talking and thinking about God is not an isolated activity, something that happens in a cocoon. There must be dialogue between the proclaimed Faith of the Church and the faith-beliefs of individuals. There is a clear link between what we believe about God and how we worship. There will always be a delicate interplay between what we believe about God and the quality and manner of our proclamation. Then, of course, our faith is vain if what we believe about God does not determine the way in which we live. The call to serve a holy God means nothing if our daily life is not shaped by the holiness of God. In that respect Methodists should hear an echo of the Methodist Church's belief that it was raised up 'to spread scriptural holiness'. On a healthy developing Christian pilgrimage, both in individual and corporate terms, there will be interplay between theology and the content of belief, between theology and the act of believing, between theology and the worship offered to God, between theology and proclamation, and between theology and the summons to the holy life.

The problem with the term 'faith' is that it has two meanings. A distinction has to be made between (i) the deposit of faith, its content, the substance of Christian belief, and (ii) having faith, the subjective stance of believers, the act of believing. There are, of course, those, even some modern theologians who, in the spirit of Harold Wilson, write disparagingly about what they regard as the secondary language of doctrinal formulation. They consider that the language of the Creeds, all propositional statement about God, leads to an over-intellectualisation and depersonalisation of the faith. We believe in a Person, not in an intellectual abstraction. However, it is the claim of this book that believing in God in itself is not enough. The notion has to have some content and just as the story the apostles told crossed the boundary between the facts of the story and their interpretation, so the modern disciple will also tell the story as he or she has received it and seek to interpret the significance of Jesus Christ for the world in which we live. Belief should make a difference to the way we live. It remains true, none the less, that the faith which is believed is a large part of our subject matter and that we cannot *do* theology without a measure of faith.

One of the Church's main tasks, some would say its prime task, is to worship God. The Church is a worshipping community. Again what the early Church felt able to say, to sing and pray in the context of worship, led to development in what they were saying about the relationship between Jesus and God. There can be little doubt that worship played a major and formative part in the development of doctrine. The growing understanding of Jesus as both human and divine was impelled by the worshipping Church's experience of his presence with them. He was invoked as well as proclaimed. He was the one in whose name they gathered (cf. 1 Corinthians 16:22 Maranatha – Our Lord has come). Examples of the way in which worship influences the shape of the Church's doctrine can be multiplied many times over.

However, with the development and refinement of the Church's teaching over the first five centuries of its life, doctrine, under constant theological scrutiny, came to play a controlling or regulating part in regard to worship. The Church's credal formularies came to be the Marquis of Queensbury rules for doing theology. They defined the area within which it could legitimately take place and indicated at what points it went beyond the bounds. Worship could no longer be offered in any other terms if it were to remain an expression of the orthodox Faith.

The Church is a worshipping people, but it is also called upon to testify to the nature and being of God and bear witness to his activity in the world. The Church has experienced the presence and activity of God in Christ on the cross and God has given to the Church the task of bearing witness to it. So the Church herself becomes a part of God's further presence and activity in the world. There is therefore a two-way interaction between theology and preaching. Theology must serve the Church's witness. This it does by helping to keep the preaching of the Church faithful to the crucified Jesus Christ. When it preaches success in the world's terms, equating it with wealth, status and a *good* job, when it collects alms for the poor on gold dishes, preaching will recall the Church to the witness of the Christ on the cross whose success is measured by his readiness to serve and to lay down his life for his friends.

Theology will serve our preaching by helping to make the witness intelligible and credible in different social contexts and cultures. That does not, of course, mean selling out to our modern culture. We have to take our cultural context seriously and as far as is consistent with the integrity of the Christian faith allow it to take root in the soil of the culture that it addresses, but the gospel may also judge our culture and find it wanting. In August of the year 2000 I went as part of a delegation to the West African Republic of Benin. We were sent there by the British Methodist Conference to try and mediate in a dispute which in spite of its many dimensions focuses in the end on who is to be the President of the Methodist

Church there and the length of his mandate. At the beginning of that mediation process I led a Bible study on the footwashing described in John 13. I read the words:

> So if I, your Lord and Teacher, have washed your feet, you also ought to wash one another's feet. For I have set you an example, that you also should do as I have done to you. Very truly, I tell you, servants are not greater than their master . . .
>
> John 13: 14-16

I repeated that Jesus had given us an example of the style and quality of leadership which he expects of us, a willingness to wash one another's feet and perform the task of a slave. So, I offered to wash the feet of the people present beginning with the youngest, which in African society would not normally be the place to begin. The youngest happened to be a woman. I washed the feet of several people until I heard the stage whisper of one of the senior Church leaders in my ear: 'This is not an African way of being a leader.' I stood up and said that I am happy to encourage the inculturisation of the gospel in African soil, to encourage African styles of worship and so on, but this was a point at which the gospel judges African culture and European culture and the world's standards of success. The gospel way of being a leader is to be a servant who like Jesus is prepared to kneel down to wash feet.

Preaching is not something that only takes place in words. It takes place in who we are, in what we say and in what we do. Our witness will be vain if our actions deny what we say with our lips. The Church is called to be holy and to embody holiness in daily life. The true understanding of what it means to take the name of the Lord our God in vain is to claim to follow Jesus Christ and to live in a manner contrary to his teaching. Again there is a two-way interaction between holiness and what we believe and proclaim about God. The responsibility of the Church to be holy will act as a check to exclude certain theological opinions, for we are called to be holy as God is holy. If a theological point of view leads to unholy living, then it can only be wrong. A Boer theology of election which leads to a political programme of apartheid could only ever be wrong. Paul's argument in Romans 6 is that the setting aside of all law – 'I have been set free to do what I like' – can only be wrong, for it contradicts the call to the life of holiness. Conversely, theological reflection can help the Church to fulfil its vocation to holy living. When difficult moral issues arise theology has a duty to bring its informed sense of duty, its understanding of the requirements of the holy life to bear on the question at issue. Is this in harmony with God's will and in line with his presence? Not everything can be settled by reference to the Scriptures. Theology has to bring the picture of God presented in Christ to inform areas of discussion which do not have simple, ready-made answers but with which we have to wrestle. Theologians must not abdicate their responsibility even when they do not speak with one voice.

Giving a reason

There are those who think that Christian faith is by definition beyond the scope of rational argument because, as one philosopher once described it, it is like making a wager and living one's life as if it is true.[10] Either God exists or he does not. If he does not exist, there is nothing to be gained from holding the belief that he does. If he does exist there is everything to be gained. However, one thing is very plain whichever side one comes down on. Neither can *prove* the truth or falsehood of the position taken up. At the end of the day we still walk by faith. Unfortunately there are some Christians who are afraid of using the mind God gave them. They somehow fear that the faith by which they live will disintegrate if they think about it too much. On the other hand if there is a God – and I am one of those who believe that there is – he is greater than anyone or anything we can conceive. We certainly will not be able to squeeze him between our ears or incarcerate him in our puny minds. He manifestly can have nothing to fear from human beings thinking about him! In this context Christians have a peg on which to hang their hat.

> Always be ready to make your defence to anyone who demands from you an accounting for the hope that is in you; yet do it with gentleness and reverence.
>
> 1 Peter 3:15-16

Giving 'an accounting for the hope that it in you' is the basis on which Christians have for centuries undertaken the apologetic task. Apologetics has nothing to do with saying sorry. It is a discipline much neglected and much needed today. It is concerned to indicate the rationality, the cogency and the coherence of the Christian Faith. The heart of the Faith may be beyond proof but it is not irrational nor anti-rational.

Nevertheless, if God is greater than anything we can conceive, then how could we know anything about him unless he were to make himself known? The primary category of knowledge for Christians is revelation – what God has made known. Reason cannot deduce from known principles what God ought to do. God is not bound. 'I will be what I will be.' We do not know all the principles. God is transcendent and ultimately unfathomable. However, when we believe God has acted, we can try to find out why he has. We can reflect on what we believe by faith. St Anselm wrote 'Cur Deus Homo', 'Why did God become a human being? – a question – or 'Why God became a human being' – a statement. Whichever, it could not have been written prior to the birth of Jesus! God has acted in becoming human. Anselm reflects on why.

Christian reasoning is reasoning *after* things have happened. Theology is based on data, information given, in the Christian case by the belief that God has acted decisively in Jesus. Theology is controlled by the object of its study. God is in charge of what we can know. Nevertheless, theology is basically an intellectual activity. It involves the ability to reason. We are beings who reason. It is not possible to do theology without using this basic human faculty and we should notice that in matters related to natural order there is no special theological presupposition. Logic is logic is logic. There is no special theological logic. One plus one plus one equals three in theology as well as in the arithmetic I learned at school. The law of gravity is the same for Christians as for anyone else. In terms of theology the created order is guaranteed by God's Word or God's Reason.

The Christian faith and thought, however, may go beyond creation, natural law and reason, that is to say, that we may have to go beyond pure reason because God transcends creation, but our faith will not be counter to reason or anti-rational, for that would create a distinction between God and his creation. He would be set against his own Word and would be involved in self-contradiction which would be plainly silly. There is a corrective use of reason in theology but our statements must not be counter to reason.

The Christian's faith may transcend reason(ing) because faith is an engagement of the whole person. Love may do unreasonable (ie. extravagant) things, but it should not be irrational. (cf. Pascal: 'The heart has its reasons which the reason may not know.') For example, suppose I were to draw out our entire life savings in order to buy my wife an anniversary present. It may be an excessive thing to do, but it may be entirely explicable. It could be understood in terms of my great love for her. The reason for the action is found in what I feel for her. It is not in the strict sense irrational, for we are capable of going beyond our rationality.

The Christian's use of reason is most closely comparable to the historian's use of it. We interpret inter-personal events rather than making impersonal deductions from axioms. We seek patterns in historical processes. However, unlike the historian in relation to history, the theologian will be looking for God's acts, for what the patterns mean in their depth in relation to God.

There is no more urgent task for Christians than the apologetic one, giving a reason for the hope that is in us, 'making a defence to anyone demands from you an accounting . . .' But we should take heed. 'Do it with gentleness and reverence . . .' Christians should not be arrogant or dismissive in the face of genuine searching. We should not shout loud and bluff when our argument is weak. We should not put our sources of authority beyond scrutiny. We should have confidence in what we believe. Faith is not believing in spite of the odds. It is believing because it makes coherent sense of life, the world, and of our own experience, which is where our human reason comes in.

The search for meaning

> Because we human beings are born and die, because we live between memory and hope, because we have some sense of unfolding human events in which we live, meaning for us will have to be structured like a story, a story that is moving toward dénouement, some telos. In brief, human meaning is usually found in narrative structures.[11]

Most people want to believe that life has some sort of meaning, that it matters whether or not they are born and live and die. To want it does not make it true, but most are not ready to believe with Shakespeare's Macbeth that:

> Life's but a walking shadow, a poor player,
> That struts and frets his hour upon the stage,
> And then is heard no more; it is a tale
> Told by an idiot, full of sound and fury,
> Signifying nothing.

Most cannot live without hope of some kind. Many seek a sense of direction, the feeling that they are going somewhere and that it is not a matter of indifference whether they do good or evil. Some seem to stumble from day to day without thinking much about anything ultimate. Others shop around amongst the world's philosophers and theologians. Some in our pick 'n mix society shop at the home-faith counter whilst yet others go to the delicatessen of world religions. In such a context the Christian Faith has to display its wares like any other purveyor of meaning. It can no longer claim a monopoly. It has to compete with everything else that is on offer.

Preachers and teachers, in fact anyone concerned to communicate the essence of Christianity, should be clear what they have to offer. First, they must invite their hearers to believe that there is one God who is best known through the life, death and resurrection of Jesus Christ and that his existence makes a difference. The heart of the gospel message is that, if we want to know what God is like, we must start with Jesus of Nazareth. Jesus witnesses to the fact that this God is to be trusted. He loves everything he has made, including each one of us. We are valued not for any utilitarian reason but in and for ourselves. The value God places upon us is that of a unique, priceless work of art. He wants to enter into relationship with each of us, out of his boundless love for us and by our free response. He invites us individually and corporately to co-operate with him in bringing the whole of creation into harmony with his will. We each have a place within that scheme of things. It is the task of Christians to seek for themselves the special contribution God has for them to make and to help others to find their place in his plans. There will always be a new thing to do to help bring about the vision of the End-time that God offers to us. This is an invitation to a life of challenge, to a life of constant change, to a life of adventure, with all kinds of risks, but one which is ultimately fulfilling. It gives a sense of purpose and significance.

> The language of our faith tells a story of a world in which new life is possible.[12]

Value, significance and purpose should not, of course, be confused with status or place-seeking. Being *somebody* is about being differentiated from the crowd and having a special contribution to make. On the occasion of my visit as President of the Methodist Conference to the Indian YMCA in London, to celebrate the 50th anniversary of the inauguration of the Church of South India, I had a reserved seat in the third row. I was due to 'bring greetings' on behalf of the Methodist Church. My wife Margaret and I sat down. Suddenly a tall, willowy lady in her 70s, clearly a refugee from the Raj, steamed up to us and said: 'Are you *somebody* sitting there?' I was determined not to say: 'I am the President of the Methodist Conference.' I rather piously said: 'Aren't we all *somebody*?' 'Well,' she rattled on, 'were you in India?' 'No,' I replied, 'all my missionary experience has been on the West Coast of Africa.' 'Well, I was in India for three years,' was the ready retort. In the end I said: 'It is obviously an oversight on somebody's part that you have not been able to find your reserved seat, please have mine and I'll go and sit over there at the side.' I moved. She took my seat but the sufferer was Margaret who had to listen to her for over two hours. We should not be worried about status. God offers us a servant role . . . a service in which we find our true selves. It is ultimately satisfying and fulfilling.

Preachers ought to remind themselves periodically of why they preach and ensure that what they say and do is rooted in the Christian Scriptures, for the biblical text acts as a mirror in which we find meaning. As David Buttrick reminds us, because we have some sense of unfolding human events in which we live, 'meaning for us will have to be structured like a story' but such a story will properly be going somewhere. Without a sense of direction the story might finally turn out to be meaningless. Our task in preaching will be to tell the story which generated our credal statements. We do that not just for its own sake but rather in order that those who hear it may experience it for themselves from the inside and find in it their own abiding importance to God.

Doctrine

Presbyters and deacons on the point of being ordained are asked (see *The Methodist Worship Book* p.303 and p.317):

> Do you believe the doctrines of the Christian faith as this Church has received them?

Those who are to be admitted to the office of local preacher are asked (see *The Methodist Worship Book* p.333):

> Will you be faithful in prayer and in the reading and study of the Scriptures, and will you preach nothing contrary to the doctrines of the Methodist Church?

The questions first and foremost ask the ordinands and the prospective local preachers to identify themselves with a Church made up of people called Methodists by affirming their recognition of and adherence to a body of doctrines 'as this Church has received them'. It is a public declaration of belonging and acceptance of the authority of the Methodist Church in a context where

> The Conference shall be the final authority within the Methodist Church with regard to all questions concerning the interpretation of its doctrines.
>
> The Methodist Church Act 1976

However, the way in which the questions are framed implicitly recognises that there are some doctrines belonging to other Churches and their doctrinal formulations which the Methodist Church does not ask its ministers and local preachers to believe or promulgate, in the belief sometimes that they do not constitute legitimate doctrinal development because interpretation has lost contact with the base-story contained in scripture. What is clear is that the language of doctrinal formulation and credal statement is used for the purposes of definition. The problem is that whereas it may be employed in stating where the *official* truth lies its immediate effect is to exclude. The more precise the definition the greater the exclusion. Yet the Methodist Church treasures its place in the Church Universal.

> The Methodist Church claims and cherishes its place in the Holy Catholic Church, which is the Body of Christ. It rejoices in the inheritance of the apostolic faith, and loyally accepts the fundamental principles of the historic Creeds and of the Protestant Reformation.

As to its doctrine, the Methodist Church states:

> (1) The doctrines of the evangelical faith, which Methodism has held from the beginning, and still holds, are based upon the divine revelation recorded in the Holy Scriptures. The Methodist Church acknowledges this revelation as the supreme rule of faith and practice. These evangelical doctrines, to which the preachers of the Methodist Church, are pledged, are contained in Wesley's *Notes on the New Testament* and the first four volumes of his Sermons.
>
> (2) The *Notes on the New Testament* and the *Forty-four Sermons* are not intended to impose a system of formal or speculative theology on Methodist preachers, but to set up standards of preaching and belief which should secure loyalty to the fundamental truths of the gospel of redemption, and to ensure the continual witness of the Church to the realities of the Christian experience of salvation.

Whilst holding to the Scriptures and the interpretation of the events surrounding the life of Jesus already contained within them, Methodists in common with all mainstream Churches also hold to the teaching emanating from the Great Councils of the Church. The writings of John Wesley are of a different kind. They 'set up standards of preaching and belief' which demonstrate how the Scriptures and the tradition of the Church may be faithfully interpreted. However, the Scriptures themselves are not an unvarnished, independent account of a series of historical events. Already within the New Testament interpretation has taken place. There is evidence, for example, in the writings of Paul about a controversy between those who wanted to enforce the requirements of the Old Covenant on the subject of circumcision and those who, like Paul, claimed that it was not necessary. This process of definition and interpretation of what God had done in Christ went on over the years in the interests of setting up standards of orthodoxy and in order to define what Christians believed. The Creeds, like much catechetical material, provide a set of pegs, ready reference points, to which both individually and corporately we can turn to find in handy summary form what the Church teaches. In the context of worship the Creeds may also have had a doxological function. They were used to bear witness to the Church's belief and as hymn-like material used in the praise of God.

Pegs, none the less, however useful, are dead wooden things unless somehow the truths they seek to express are brought to life. Handing on to a new generation a dead system or a set of one-line assertions will achieve little if the truth of what is affirmed is not discovered in individual and corporate experience. Every doctrine needs a periodic MOT test to find out if it is still in working order.

> No matter how correct one's theology is in any generation, it makes no difference if it is not translated into its own time and cultural perspective . . . Atonement, sanctification, Trinity – all fine theological shorthand must be translated because the 21st century world knows not the stories from which they came.[13]

There is in our society today an abysmal ignorance of basic biblical teaching, which can be a wonderful opportunity to tell again the basic story of Jesus free from the clutter of past cultural accretion. However, those who tell the story need to be aware of the points at which the account of what Jesus said and did slides over into interpretation of it. It is the interpretation which grows and develops, initially coming to a climax in the middle of the fifth century of the Christian era, but going on down to the present day. The Christian preacher should be as informed as possible about the history of theology over the centuries. A knowledge of the early Councils, some understanding of the paradigm shift at the time of the Reformation, some awareness of the modern attacks on faith from science and philosophy, will enrich us personally as preachers and be a mine of illustration about how men and women have experienced God with them down the ages.

> . . . Christianity as a whole, whatever individual Christians may feel to be possible for them, cannot live without a constant and serious dialogue with its own ever-growing tradition.[14]

The basic thesis in what follows is that Christian doctrine is not the perverse invention of philosophers and theologians but the distillation of what those who first encountered Jesus of Nazareth came to believe about him and his relationship with God. The task of preachers is therefore to help their hearers discover the truth of that doctrine in their own experience. In short, doctrine has to become experience once again. That will mean beginning with the story of how a man came up to a group of fisherfolk and invited them to follow him, how they journeyed with him until they discovered that he was indeed the Christ and Son of the living God. The Anglican Report *Christian Believing* is right when it says:

> The classical structure of a credal sentence is neither simply 'We believe in . . .' nor 'We believe that . . .', but 'We believe in . . . who . . .'[15]

The focus of Christian preaching is a person whose life was interpreted in such ways that a body of doctrine grew on top of it. That interpretation is to be treated seriously. What began as experience must be expounded so that it becomes experience again. As a textbook for local preachers of a former generation declares, doctrinal preaching should make the preacher and the congregation think.

> But, if preaching does no more than this, it will have failed of its true purpose. It should make them *see* and *feel* the great beliefs of our faith, and it should prompt them to *action* as well.[16]

Its supreme task is to speak of Jesus Christ and the principle vehicle for doing this will be through the telling of stories.

2

THE USE OF STORY

In 1948 I was ten. One day I was left in charge of my brother and two sisters – with dire warnings about what would happen if we didn't behave – whilst mum went to Bunker's shop round the corner. She wouldn't be gone long but it was enough time for me to discover in a drawer a packet of sparklers, bought in for Bonfire Day. 'I'll show you how they work,' I said, sticking one through the bars of the grate into the glowing embers of the fire. (We didn't have a fire-guard. Only middle-class people had fire-guards in those days!) The sparkler began to splutter. I waved it about my head and ran through into the scullery where the sparks caught on a sticky 'flies' cemetery'. The whole thing went up in a sheet of flame. I dropped the sparkler into the stone sink and, with my brother, filled milk bottles with water. We stood underneath the burning flycatcher, legs spread wide, and with a double-handed hold threw water up into the air at the flames. The water went nowhere near the target. It fell back on top of us and ran all over the floor.

In the meantime my youngest sister Margaret'd run out of the front door, shouting: 'John's got the house on fire!' She got the attention of old Mr Kitchen from the end of the row, deaf as a post, who arrived at the back gate with a ladder. He was going to rescue us from

> burning upstairs windows, but he couldn't get through the back gate. It was jammed shut with a full dustbin behind it. Anyway, the fire was out. So Mr Kitchen was persuaded that everything was all right and he went away.
>
> Well, what were we to do? Mum'ud kill us. So, we decided to get some lime from the shed – Dad was a quarryman, so there was always some lime there – and we mixed a bucket of whitewash. I stood on top of a hard wooden chair and tried to paint the ceiling. Well, the whitewash just ran down the brush handle, down my arm, all over me and made a growing puddle on the floor. A few grey streaks touched the big sooty black patch on the ceiling. We were just making a bigger mess. So, we wiped it up as best we could and then we heard the front door go. Mother was back. We all rushed and sat in a line in descending order of height, like the Horlicks advert, (or was it Ovaltine – I don't remember now), and sat rigid with arms firmly folded. She walked through the door, saw us bolt upright, very still and she said: 'What've ye done?' And I didn't sit down for a fortnight.

It makes a good story, especially when told with dramatic gestures, waving the right arm with the sparkler, throwing the water with a two-handed hold on the milk bottle, legs apart and knees bent, painting the ceiling and illustrating how the whitewash ran down my arm. Folding arms, like in the advert, will elicit firm information as to whether it *was* Horlicks or Ovaltine. If I wanted to tell that story in a public context it wouldn't be difficult to find a 'flies' cemetery' (a sticky flycatcher) and a milk bottle to bring it dramatically to life. It is told when the family meets. It only takes a brief reference: 'Do you remember when you set the house on fire . . . ?' Our faces are soon wreathed in smiles. There are gales of laughter as the comic picture of deaf old Mr Kitchen with his ladder pushing against the dustbin to get the gate open is conjured up once again. The story belongs to us and occasionally it gets embellished a bit in the telling, honed to polish it for the next time it's told. Soon it isn't easy any longer to swear to the exact and precise accuracy of each detail. It cannot be told by anyone else to the same effect. It is a trivial story. It has no great inner meaning to be discovered. It has no overarching significance. But it is *our* story and together with other stories like it, some sad, some joyful it makes us a family. It is our sharing of the story that invests a past, isolated incident with meaning. Whereas taken on its own it might well have no significance at all, the retelling of the story binds us together in such a way that the story itself lives. It is in places even embellished by us in the interests of having a good story to tell. What is true of my family and your family is true of our faith communities.

Overarching story

The story of the Exodus and the Exile creates a people. The Jews have a shared narrative which makes them a family, a family which has known slavery and liberation from captivity, conquest and restoration. Without the stories of Abraham and Sarah, Isaac and Rebekah, Jacob-Israel, Leah and Rachel, without Joseph, Moses and Miriam, and a fierce generation of prophets, without poets, priests, lawmakers and interpreters of the Law, this doggedly independent people would have remained a disparate group of nomads. It was belief in the God of Moses which made them a nation. But sometimes they lost their grip on their own history and they were faithless and unbelieving. So God sent the prophets with dire warnings about the consequences of losing touch with him. Hosea's son, Lo-ammi, becomes a walking message. His very name bears a warning, 'for you are not my people and I am not your God'.[17] It is possible to lose contact with the story and to be excluded from it. On the other hand, it is the fact that God has saved a rabble of slaves from bondage in Egypt that makes them a people. Even their apostasy is absorbed into the ongoing recital of their common history. It too helps to create their national identity.

The problem we have today, we are told, is that in our postmodern world there is no 'metanarrative'. There is no overarching story which gives meaning to the whole and creates a common identity. In our pick 'n mix society people take a little here and a little there and make their own personal package, to suit themselves in their individual need. Eastern mysticism is mingled with aromatherapy, reflexology and a sense of belonging to Mother Earth. Or choose any selection of your own. Suit yourself. Be yourself, as if that is possible alone. For worship, if you feel disposed, choose a touch of Taizé, an inch of Iona; then add a few choruses to taste. Believe what you can, if you can. The trouble is that there is no community to match the varied selected packages, so that we have a generation which believes almost anything but has little or no sense of belonging. There is no common story that binds people together. There is therefore no sense of obligation, no agreed framework. 'Thou shalt' or even 'Thou shalt not . . .' becomes 'Do your own thing. Be yourself.' It is in so doing that you will 'get a life'. But does it really have to be so? Do we not have a choice?

The very premises undergirding postmodernist thinking ought to mean that we can opt for the Jesus-story, or any part of it, if we wish. It is unlikely that for the world at large the story of Jesus will, in such a climate, be chosen in its entirety by the community in which we live as its metanarrative, to provide its overarching sense of identity. Yet it remains possible and plausible that we may be grasped by the story and find ourselves belonging to a para-community, which challenges the standards and norms of the society in the midst of which we live. Being Church has always had the feel of being called out of the world around, offering an alternative to the prevailing climate of opinion. So, the Church may, indeed ought, to tell the story which gives Christian meaning. It is the story of the life and ministry, the death, resurrection and ascension of Jesus of Nazareth, whom his first followers proclaimed as the expected Messiah. We have to tell it in establishing our communal Christian identity.

Within the wider Christian family there are indeed sub-sets which have a subsidiary story to tell. Methodists become a 'tribe' within the larger Church by telling the story of the Anglican priest John Wesley whom they believe God raised up as the instrument of the great revival of religion in the 18th century. They tell the story of his 'heart-warming' which took place at about 'a quarter before nine' on the evening of 24th May 1738. They talk about and sing the hymns of his brother Charles. Stories about how John was rescued from the Rectory fire in Epworth are told to emphasise that God had reserved for him a special role. However, even within the Methodist grouping there are sub-stories, stories about Primitive Methodist heroes like Hugh Bourne and William Clowes, which bind a group-within-a-group to a common identity, tradition and way of doing things. Sometimes memory is exercised selectively with the intention of excluding one group or another. Their story is not remembered and not kept alive, in order to indicate that that group no longer exists or is a part of our history that we want to leave behind. If, however, we are to understand where we have come from we need to tell the whole story, for these stories too are a part of who we are today.

Resonance and dissonance

To hear a story which does not remind us of something is not a story that we are likely to remember. The best stories are those which provide hooks on which to hang some part of our experience. They help to make sense of something that we experienced in the past and which we did not understand at the time. A new link is made. A moment of insight occurs. 'The penny drops,' as we say. Yet, generally speaking, it only happens because the 'discovery' is consonant with the life experience of the one who is grasped by this new perspective.

> The preacher . . . does not essentially tell people what they do not already know, so much as show them the meaning and depth of their own experience. He calls them to stop,

> look and listen, to see what God is doing in their midst.[18]

As Christine Pilkington wrote in the second volume of this series:

> Resonances of meaning are not something invented in thc last few decades, but something common to the interpretation of texts over the millennia.[19]

The vibrations set up at the point of impact of a story can spread out from its epicentre to produce after-shocks a long way away. It can rattle the window-frames of those through whose eyes and ears the story is passed on.

Consider the following story told by Thomas G Long under the heading *The Good News about Sin*:

> One morning while leaving preaching class, a student asked if she could discuss a matter with me. We grabbed a cup of coffee and sat down to talk. Her problem, she said, was that she was working on a sermon based on a biblical text about God's judgement, and she was having a struggle. 'I can preach love and I can preach hope and grace,' she said, 'but I cannot bring myself to preach about sin and judgement. There are already too many bad messages out there in people's lives, and I don't want to add one more burden.'
>
> We talked this matter over for a few minutes, aiming at no particular resolution and arriving at none. Then she changed the subject. Her teenage son, she told me, was giving her family problems. He had gotten hooked on drugs, had been suspended from school, and was terrorising the whole family. He came and went as he pleased, commandeering the car, taking money where he could find it, threatening his parents with

> his abusive speech. My student told me that her husband's response to this was to retreat into depression. She began to cry, thinking about the situation.
>
> 'Last night,' she said, 'I finally broke down. My son blew into the house and after hurling angry words at his dad and me, slammed the door to his room. I decided that enough was enough, and I went back there. I admit I am afraid of him. My son is over six feet tall and big, and I was unsure of what he might do physically. But I opened the door, stood in the doorway, looked him directly in the eye, and said with all the firmness in my being, 'I love you so much I will not allow you to do this to yourself or to us anymore.'
>
> We sat there for a moment, her words of the night before still hanging in the air. 'I think I have just heard,' I finally said, 'a powerful and faithful sermon on sin and judgement.'[20]

A powerful story, but its impact is more immediate the nearer one is to the experience. I have transmitted to you something I read in a book about preaching. The story there was told by an American professor writing about someone in one of his classes who at the end of the lecture says: 'May I have a word?' I recognise that situation because people have in my time said after class: 'May I have a word?' That, however, is not the heart of the experience. We are invited through the professor to listen to a private conversation about what happened in the student's home. She describes the havoc, the unhappiness, caused by her son. It does not take a great act of imagination to feel her and her husband's sense of helplessness and anger and frustration as their son interprets the word 'freedom' in terms of his own capacity for doing exactly what he likes, until that point of utter desperation is reached when she digs in her toes and says: 'I love you so much I will not allow you to do this to yourself or to us anymore.' That is the punch-line of her story. That is what happened in her home. It is about her love for her son.

The university professor has, however, a slightly different agenda. On the basis of the student's experience he wants her to appreciate that she does in fact know what it means to preach about sin and judgement. So in the ante-room of the student's story, at one remove from what happened between a son and his parents, the professor makes his point. 'I think I have just heard a powerful and faithful sermon on sin and judgement.' This too resonates with my experience, firstly because I know the teacher/preacher's temptation to make the point in case it should be missed, and secondly because I have a son who once was like that.

This is a story I tell with permission, but then I have had the space to ask permission. I hope that the American professor's story was told at least with the permission of his student who needed to unburden herself, if not with the permission of her son. In fact, I have two sons. One has never given us a real day's trouble since the day he was born. The second for years hardly gave us a day's peace of mind. In his early teens he looked like a blond lavatory brush. He brought home successive girlfriends of the era when they dressed all in black, looking as if they had dropped out of the trees, with hair all round, so that you did not know which side was looking at you. It was impossible to talk to him. Any attempt at communication was shouted down. Out he would go with the loud banging of doors. He smoked. He drank under age and we wondered if the next knock at the door would be the police. He drove us to desperation. Things reached such a pitch that I sat down and wrote him a long letter telling him in precise terms exactly what he was doing to us. I left it in his room but he never mentioned it.

Then the point came where I had to move from Birmingham to London and we thought that this would be the natural break-point, the parting of the ways. He was 18 and we could think of no obvious reason why he should want to move with us, but to our astonishment he said that he *was* moving with us. We did not know whether to be pleased or not.

He had never found difficulty in finding work. He is intelligent. Within 24 hours of arrival he was again in paid employment and almost overnight he became a model son, well nearly. His room, which before the move had been the ultimate tip, suddenly became the cleanest place in the house. Whereas his mother's cooking had previously been called slops, suddenly it became the source of compliments and thanks. When this lasted until Christmas, we prayed: 'O Lord, can we have an extension to Easter, please?' The only conclusion we could reach was that he had not known in Birmingham how to separate himself from his so-called friends, who certainly in the longer term turned out to be no friends at all. Our move gave him an acceptable reason for his break with them. The temporary conclusion of this part of his journey was reached – it can never be an end, for his story continues – when he came downstairs from his room with the letter in which I had poured out our pain. 'You can have it back now,' he said.

The story of my son is not the same as the story told by Professor Long's student, but it has sufficient family resemblance for me to feel the vibrations. Her story resonates with mine. I can feel the oppressive weight of despair and anger and frustration which she was carrying because I have been there. I've got the T-shirt. Human beings find help and comfort in recognising their own experience in other people's stories. It helps to know that we are not alone and that we are not the only ones to have travelled this road. However, for the Christian preacher telling such a story there has to be a reference point. We do not tell stories because we just happen to have heard a story, dragging it screaming into a context with which it has no natural links. We do not offer a story in isolation. Christian preaching may through the telling of a story be good therapy, a piece of psychological cleansing, but however good that may be in itself, it is a rather hit-and-miss affair, for by telling a story no preacher can guarantee that there will be set up any vibrations at all within the hearer's experience. It just so happens that I can recognise some elements of my experience in her story.

Professor Long's intention in describing what happened in his conversation with his student was to demonstrate that she did know something about preaching sin and judgement. It is clear, however, that I picked up a different set of vibrations from the ones intended, or perhaps it would be better to say 'in addition to' what was intended. The story set other bells ringing which echoed with another story arising out of my own knowledge of the Scriptures, namely of the parable of Jesus commonly called the Parable of the Prodigal Son. So, for me, the train of thought set in motion by a story told for one purpose, resonated in triangular fashion with my own experience and a Bible story, to speak volumes about estrangement, judgement and return and to speak of a parent's enduring love in spite of the child's behaviour. That goes beyond the student's description of life with her son, for stories often take on a life of their own. Preachers should always have a clear purpose in telling a story but know at the same time that it will move beyond their control, which may be the space in which the Holy Spirit may do more than we intend.

One of the fundamental problems that preachers have today is that our contemporaries do not know the narrative framework of the gospel. Casual references to the Pearl of Great Price, the Unjust Steward, the Great Assize – or any other random choice – are not likely to be understood, even in the context of public worship.

> In that sense, one of our major tasks as preachers is probably simply to tell the story.[21]

People will identify with what rings true in their own experience. It may be also that additional illustration of how it rang true in someone else's experience may set up an even wider field of resonance so that when someone in the Church porch says: 'You know when you said . . . it made me think of . . .' the story has taken on a life of its own. Story is not the precise language of philosophical definition. It is far too allusive and indirect. It invites the hearer to step onto the stage and get involved in the action and to influence the direction that the story will take.

> The story is more than a piece of information. It is an invitation to people to identify the story, to identify their own stories, and if they wish to step into the story and be participants in it. Many who went to see the musical *Godspell* were surprised to find themselves invited onto the stage at the interval to mix with the performers. That is what a story is meant to do.[22]

However, as well as setting up positive vibrations a story may have the effect of bringing us up sharp in our tracks. It may constitute a serious challenge to what we think and to the way in which we behave. The classic example of such a story is found in 2 Samuel 12:1-15, where the prophet Nathan visits King David to tell him about a man who possessed many flocks and herds, whilst his poor neighbour only had 'one little ewe lamb, which he had bought' (v3). It was really a family pet. However, when the rich man had a visitor, rather than take one of his own flock, he took the poor man's lamb and served it up to his guest.

David was incensed to hear of this outrage and threatened the perpetrator with death. Then came the slap in the face. 'You are the man!' said Nathan. He hit David between the eyes with the news that God's judgement was upon him, for God had given him many wives and many possessions. Yet he had taken the wife of Uriah the Hittite and put Uriah in the hottest part of the forthcoming battle to ensure that Bathsheba, his wife, would soon be a widow. There was no doubt that David got the message.

There can be no question but that from time to time we all need to be challenged in our smugness, complacency, self-satisfaction and blindness. There are times enough when we see the splinter in the eye of someone else and do not recognise the railway sleeper in our own. Sometimes it is necessary for preachers, in the name of God – never merely for their own satisfaction – to offer rebuke. It will not be a weekly occurrence, for congregations will soon react if they are constantly beaten over the head. If it should be necessary it will best be done with humour which helps everyone to find a sense of proportion.

The prophet Amos may not have employed much in the way of humour, but he understood the psychological make-up of his hearers. He begins his tirade against injustice by announcing God's terrible judgement, successively, on Damascus, Gaza, Tyre, Edom, Ammon and Moab. The people love it. All their enemies come in for it. They listen slavering with the enjoyment of hearing their enemies put in their place.

> Thus says the LORD: For three transgressions of Damascus, and for four, I will not revoke the punishment; because they have threshed Gilead with threshing sledges of iron. So I will send a fire on the house of Hazael, and it shall devour the strongholds of Ben-hadad. I will break the gate bars of Damascus, and cut off the inhabitants from the Valley of Aven, and the one who holds the sceptre from Beth-eden; and the people of Aram shall go into exile to Kir, says the LORD.[23]

Amos gives an account of their wickedness and pronounces God's judgement. 'Thus says the LORD . . .'

Then the congregation becomes a little uneasy when he turns his attention to Judah, but that is still someone else's territory. Now the prophet has them ready for his hammer-blow, God's judgement upon them, 'because they sell the righteous for silver, and the needy for a pair of sandals . . .' (Amos 2:6). The indictment is terrible. In the light of what God has done for them they are without excuse. The story of the misdeeds of others, which they were enjoying, prepares the way for rebuking the people of Israel for their own.

The jarring note of a story told to rebuke should be rarely heard. It should not be used as a means of speaking to an individual who ought to be addressed face to face. It may properly be heard as a challenge to the attitudes of the church-community, seeking to hone its vision. It may be addressed to the world at large to question its standards. Whichever . . . the preacher too will certainly be included in the scope of the judgement, if this is truly the word of God to all.

The parable-jokes of Jesus

> To you has been given the secret of the kingdom of God, but for those outside, everything comes in parables; in order that 'they may indeed look, but not perceive, and may indeed listen, but not understand; so that they may not turn again and be forgiven'.[24]

> With many such parables he spoke the word to them, as they were able to hear it: he did not speak to them except in parables, but he explained everything in private to his disciples.[25]

On the surface at least these words from the evangelist are some of the most difficult to interpret in the entire New Testament. It sounds as if Jesus conveyed his message in parables in order to be deliberately difficult . . . 'in order that "they may indeed look, but not perceive, and may indeed listen, but not understand"'. Such a statement feels plainly absurd. After all Jesus was clearly an exceptionally gifted teacher. How could he possibly go out of his way to make what was said hard to understand? Truly great teachers have the knack of making complicated and profound issues astoundingly simple. Whatever else this quotation may mean it cannot possibly mean that Jesus wanted to hide his real meaning from his hearers.

> No indeed; if that impression is given, it is simply due to the Hebrew tendency to express a consequence as though it were a purpose. Isaiah volunteers to be God's messenger to his people, and God takes him at his word, but says to him in effect, 'Go and deliver my message, but don't expect them to pay any attention to it . . .'[26]

There can, however, be little dispute that Jesus in his proclamation of the kingdom shows no desire to set his teaching above dispute. There is no attempt to enforce a hearing or wear his listeners down with the onslaught of irresistible logic. He offered an indication of what it is like when God is in charge. 'The kingdom of God is like . . .' and left the possibility of free response to the crazy standards of the kingdom. Some responded and some did not. No one was overwhelmed. The approach he adopted seems to have been, in the words of Johnston R McKay, 'tangential, evocative, indirect'.

> He told stories. He used metaphors. He employed parables. He was ambiguous.[27]

McKay is clearly of the opinion that Jesus' own way of teaching was soon reshaped.

> The early Church turned the ambiguous, parabolic teaching of Jesus, with its hints and signals and glimpses into reality into direct, doctrinal statements . . .[28]

Story is not the language of dogmatic definition, but it does evoke response. However, the process of reflection on the story of Jesus, his life, his ministry and his death could not be avoided in the light of the belief that God had raised him from the dead. The first followers of Jesus were bound to ask questions about the significance of what they had experienced in the company of Jesus because they had come to believe that he was still with them. None the less Jesus himself told stories in the full knowledge that many would hear and not understand, as the prophet Isaiah had warned. He knew well that story is eminently more memorable than a set of abstract philosophical propositions but that what he had to say still sounded to many enigmatic and was not immediately understood. In fact 'for those outside everything comes in parables' may mean in the spirit of the Old Testament that although the disciples know the secrets of the kingdom, to others he comes across as talking in riddles.

It is one of the greatest treasures of the Christian Church that the fundamental expression of its faith is contained in stories and not in abstruse theories. It was inevitable that the first believers should clarify what had happened in the life of Jesus, spelling out the meaning of the events and producing precise definition in the interest of establishing what it is proper to believe and what it is not. Some of this reflection itself took place in story form. How much more memorable is the story of Christmas with its angelic messengers coming to the Virgin Mary than an abstract statement about the purity of the pre-existent Christ and the theological necessity that he should be spotless from birth . . !

> Preaching narrative texts – stories of various kinds – is interesting and risky but consistent with good theology and good communication. It is consistent with good theology and communication because of the importance of indirection, openness, and the narrative form both of the Old Testament stories and of the Christian sermon.[29]

The early Church, the followers of the new Way, also inherited the Jewish Scriptures and found there a body of stories. It was the Bible on which they had been nourished. It was the Bible of Jesus. This collection of books gave an account of God's dealings with his people in narrative form. The stories of the Book of Genesis, for example, convey in simple story form truths about our human condition that it would take volumes of philosophical debate to wrestle with them. Furthermore, a story remembered because of its dramatic effect need not be understood immediately. The story may be recalled months, maybe years afterwards, perhaps in the light of another experience, when suddenly the penny drops. There is a flash of insight and in a moment it is understood. Speculative argument does not have the same grip upon us as a story simply told. Jesus told stories and it was a stroke of genius that he should have done so. The story is so much easier to remember, whereas an intricate argument simply gets us embroiled in ever greater obscurity. It is from the Old Testament treasure house that Jesus himself took the form of the parable, the riddle or enigmatic pronouncement. It is because the parables of Jesus are like jokes that we either get it or we don't get it and no amount of explanation will make it otherwise.

If you have ever had the experience of telling a story that you think is funny and nobody has laughed, you will know what a painful experience it is! It is very embarrassing and the trouble is that if you try to explain you only make matters worse. The parables of Jesus are just like that. At the end of the Parable of the Sower, Jesus says: 'Let anyone with ears to hear listen!' It's almost as if he said: 'Have you got it?' The story either hits you between the ears with its meaning – its impact is direct – or else it really is like a joke that misfires, which for me is why the explanation of the parable in the verses which follow is so tedious. We have very few examples of Jesus giving any explanation of his stories, so that one cannot help wondering if this is the evangelist explaining the joke.

For me, it is because of the similarity of the parable to a joke that I find it hard to preach on the parables. They are such wonderful examples of the storyteller's art that any attempt to retell them is likely to destroy them. They are told with a marvellous economy of words so that elaboration of them may lead to them being treated as allegories, with every bit being interpreted. The point of the parable, the punch-line, the joke element, is either grasped – and therefore needs no explanation – or else it is explained and destroyed. Looking and not perceiving, listening and not understanding may mean that there were many who heard Jesus who just did not get it, but whether they understood at the time or not, they still had the parable, the story waiting in the wings, within easy recall, which may yet be understood in the future, at some other time, in another context, when the penny would drop. His hearers had his parable-jokes.

What was so different about the disciples who had 'been given the secret of the kingdom of God'? It is very simple really. The people at large had the parables; the disciples had Jesus himself. The teaching of Jesus centred on the kingdom of God. The kingdom of God is like . . . a mustard seed, a merchant looking for pearls, someone who finds buried treasure, and so one could go on. In each of these word-pictures some aspect of the truth about God's reign is revealed. Yet in the first three gospels there is a strange tension in Jesus' teaching about the kingdom. In some sense it is already here. The kingdom is in the midst of you. In some sense it is still to be brought in. Jesus' disciples are taught to pray: 'Thy kingdom come . . .' – future. Furthermore the kingdom is in the process of being realised. The parables about the growth of seed illustrate that. That is all very confusing until we realise that God's future kingdom is embodied in Jesus. He was the one in whom the future kingdom was already present. The messenger had become the message.

The arrival of the kingdom is proclaimed in the teaching of Jesus but the disciples did not follow him because of what he *said* about the kingdom. If we look hard enough we can find parallels of almost everything he said in other places, in Jewish teaching and in the surrounding culture. But Jesus did not just talk about the kingdom; he lived it. He was the embodiment of his own teaching. In the end the disciples followed him because they met a convincing harmony of his thought and his person. Jesus' teaching did not set the world on fire simply because of its obvious superiority over any other theoretical programme. Jesus himself was the attraction. It was in him that they put their trust.

The people had parables. So did the disciples. There is precious little evidence of them seeing and understanding any better than the people at large. 'Lord, tell us what this parable *means* . . .' They did not get it. They did not understand the point of it. It was not by their intellectual assent that the disciples were any better than anybody else. It was by the exercise of the imagination that intuitively they recognised in Jesus the living demonstration of what it means to be under the rule of God. This shift in the gospel narrative was to be very significant. Modern preachers will be committed to telling stories to express the truths about the Jesus who became the message itself and, what is yet more difficult, to embodying the kingdom in their own lives.

Humour

There is one respect in which I find most of the traditional portraits of Jesus, descriptions of his life and character, almost totally deficient. That is in their failure to recognise in him any sense of humour. So often he is presented as the pale Galilean, the Man of Sorrows. Such portrayals undoubtedly safeguard a necessary part of our knowledge of him, but they cannot be the whole story. This was a man who liked to go to a party and we find shafts of humour in his preaching and conversation. We fail to do justice to him if we leave out the twinkle in his eye, but then in so doing I am exercising another gift, the imagination, when I see him smiling. Think what he said about the rich.

> . . . it is easier for a camel to go through the eye of a needle than for someone who is rich to enter the kingdom of God.
>
> Matthew 19:24

Very serious scholars with lots of degrees after six years of training in high-powered universities and membership of many learned societies have tried to ease matters for the wealthy by suggesting that perhaps one of the gates of Jerusalem was known popularly as Needle's Eye Gate, and although it would be a bit of a squeeze for an ungainly animal like a camel, with a bit of manoeuvre it would probably just about be able to get through! Or by altering the Greek text of the verse by one letter the 'camel' would become 'a thick rope', as if it would make any difference. A heavy rope would be just as much a problem as a camel! Surely it is simpler to recognise the saying as a wonderfully funny cartoon, which is remembered because of the very incongruity of it. What better cartoons could one find than the pernickety Pharisees straining out a gnat from their soup and swallowing a camel. Or yet again, someone trying with the corner of his or her hankie to remove a speck of dust from a friend's eye whilst they had a railway sleeper in their own eye. We would be set free from the plague of literalism if only we had enough imagination to see the sparkle in Jesus' eye and recognise the preacher's hyperbole as he says:

> For truly I tell you, if you have faith the size of
> a mustard seed, you will say to this mountain,
> 'Move here to there,' and it will move . . .
>
> Matthew 17:20

How many mountains have we moved from one place to another? Is the failure just because of our awesome lack of faith? Surely we would all be delivered from hundred weights of guilt if we were to see here an example of Jesus' humour which sets incongruous things beside each other, in this case a tiny mustard seed and a great big mountain.

As in the case of Jesus, in our storytelling, our utterances will be the better remembered if they have the right admixture of humour. It can, of course, like many human abilities be misused or lead to misunderstanding if not properly supervised. In Christian preaching humour should be integral to what is being said and not a pointless intervention because the preacher happens to notice that the congregation is getting bored. Its overuse may lead to people thinking that the practitioner is flippant, shallow and lightweight, which is what Mr Wesley feared, I believe, when in his *Twelve Rules of a Helper*, he writes:

> Be serious . . . . Let your motto be 'Holiness to the Lord'. Avoid all lightness, jesting, and foolish talking.

Nor should humour be used as a weapon. It is sometimes called repartee when someone is in fact being sliced up and made to look small. Positively it is the ability to recognise the incongruous and the absurd. A A Thomson tells the story of a British prisoner of war in a Japanese camp during World War Two who received a letter forwarded from home from his Income Tax Office telling him that if he did not pay his arrears forthwith he would end up in prison! Indignation against incompetent officials would not be an appropriate response. A good hearty laugh might well be.

Laughter (*with* not *at*) can be an effective social cement, provide a release of tension and help us to see things in a proper perspective. It can provide an acceptable means of self-criticism and, used sparingly, as I have already indicated, be a means of offering rebuke. A right sense of humour can be a protection against excess, for the fanatic does not know how to laugh. It can foster humility and lessen the bitterness of failure. Humour is capable of being a great healing agent. We have, I believe, the authority of Jesus himself to enliven our preaching with its use.

Imagination

> Preaching is Christian faith explaining itself anew with imagination and precision.[30]

In David Buttrick's definition the word 'precision' is necessary, for the imagination, valuable as it is, cannot simply be allowed to float off into the stratosphere. The imagination can, of course, take us on long journeys more swiftly than any jet. All we have to do is close our eyes and we can be in the midst of the most impenetrable jungle, for it is possible through the imagination to go where physically we may never go in reality. Therein lies the problem. The imagination can take us on flights of fantasy and lead us to run away from the grim realities of the world in which we live. It can, however, be the gift of insight into the way that different situations work out and other people react. At its best it is the capacity for stepping outside our own shell to feel what others feel. It can be the creative capacity for stepping inside someone else's story. It is, I believe, a wonderful gift in studying and preaching the scriptural message.

Preaching with imagination does not mean taking a flight of fantasy. The precision that is required with regard to the preacher's imagination is not allowing the imagination to claim something that cannot be legitimated out of the biblical text. Perhaps this is best expressed through an example, using an idea that is found repeatedly in the teaching of Jesus, namely that in order to enter the kingdom of God we have to become childlike. Gerd Theissen in *The Shadow of the Galilean* demonstrates how an imaginative construct can be combined with very careful, serious and critical study.

> Unless you become like children again, you will not enter the kingdom of God.

This is incorporated into the story of a merchant-contemporary of Jesus, who learns about him as he travels the land in the course of his business.[31]

> It was already late. We had to set off if we were to get to Bethsaida in time. We trotted slowly along the shore on our asses. The Sea of Galilee glittered in the sunshine. The mountains rose up from it like pale shadows. It was a peaceful afternoon. Suddenly the beggar children whom we had met at the toll gate emerged. They held out their hands and barred our way. 'What are you doing?' I asked. 'We're playing at toll collectors.' 'What frontier is this?' 'This is the beginning of the kingdom of God.' I wanted to explode with anger, but I restrained myself. Why shouldn't I play their game? So I did. 'What

must I do to enter into your kingdom?' The children laughed. The oldest one said:

'Unless you become like children again, you will not enter the kingdom of God'.
'Who rules in your kingdom?'
'We rule in this kingdom. The children. The kingdom of God is ours.'
'And what duty must I pay?'
'Give us something to eat.'
'Is that all?'
'There is no kingdom you can enter so easily. All you must do is give away what you possess. Then you belong to it.'

I didn't know whether it was a game or in real earnest. I said:
'All right. Here is the duty for your kingdom.' And I gave them a couple of loaves of bread and some fruit. Their faces shone. They gave way. We were allowed to pass. We had crossed this frontier as well.

So, preachers should bring to their study of the Scriptures the minds God gave them. They must themselves be committed students, however long they have been preaching. They must feed and stimulate their own minds and imagination by enlarging their own experience, perhaps through travel, through the arts, through reading – and not just theology. If they themselves are in these terms rich, they will have wealth to share with others. They might then hope to fire the imagination of others, for it is through the imagination as well as through the intellect that we make the connections which enable us to be grasped by the truth of the open secrets of the kingdom.

3

THE WAY INTO THE STORY

At the heart of Christian faith there is a story, which over the centuries became a body of belief. It began with a group of fishermen sitting mending their nets by the lakeside. Suddenly a man appeared and said: 'Follow me, and I will make you fish for people.'[32] And for some unaccountable reason they did precisely that. They left their nets and followed him. We aren't told why. In spite of the speculations of generations of preachers, some of them more plausible than others, in the gospel text no explanation is given of the odd fact that they did as they were told. They followed him, and in terms of the story which constitutes the identity of the present-day Christian community, that following becomes a contemporary requirement. In the words of Albert Schweitzer:

> He comes to us as One unknown, without a name, as of old, by the lake-side, He came to those men [sic] who knew Him not. He speaks to us the same word: 'Follow thou me!' and sets us to the tasks which He has to fulfil for our time. He commands. And to those who obey Him, whether they be wise or simple, He will reveal Himself in the toils, the conflicts, the sufferings which they shall pass through in His fellowship, and, as an ineffable mystery, they shall learn in their own experience Who He is.[33]

Of course, when Simon and Andrew, James and John saw this man Jesus of Nazareth approach there were no upper case letters introducing the pronouns which described him. They saw a *man*. We cannot even be sure that at that point they knew his name. They certainly did not see the Messiah, the Christ, approaching. They did not say: 'Oh, look, here comes a son/the Son of God!', with or without a capital letter. They saw a man. It was only as they followed that they discovered first of all that he was a very extraordinary person. Everyone recognised his extraordinary gifts as a preacher. He spoke as if he knew what he was talking about. He spoke with authority, a personal authority which did not make constant appeal to written sources. He spoke as one who knew himself the truth of what he was saying. His personal magnetism drew people to hear what he had to say. He was a gifted teacher who expressed himself through witty sayings, striking proverbs and maxims, and his carefully crafted stories employing everyday images grasped his hearers' attention. There can be little doubt also that he possessed a remarkable gift of healing. Simon, Andrew, James, John and the others who followed saw for themselves how people came to him with all kinds of sickness and went away healed. This Jesus of Nazareth was indeed a very special person, a charismatic preacher and healer, whose authority lay in his own person, although that is not quite how he put it himself. He believed that God himself was his authority to speak. It was not conferred on him by any office. He was in today's terms a layperson, not a priest, who earned the title Rabbi by virtue of his knowledge of the Hebrew Scriptures and the self-evident, self-authenticating truth of what he said. All of this the first disciples discovered as they travelled with him.

Jesus' self-understanding

Jesus is portrayed at the beginning of the first three gospels as someone in search of self-understanding and a sense of purpose. His self-enquiry about who he is and the nature of his mission are described in the accounts of his baptism at the hands of John the Baptist and the story of his temptation by the devil. The synoptic gospels do not present him as someone who knows with absolute certainty that he has a divine mission. We are allowed inside his mind to share his thinking as he wrestles with who he is. He accepts baptism from John and as he comes up out of the water,

> suddenly the heavens were opened to him and he saw the Spirit of God descending like a dove and alighting on him. And a voice from heaven said, 'This is my Son, the Beloved, with whom I am well pleased.'[34]

Overwhelmed with this sense of destiny he went into the desert to ask himself in what way his mission is to be fulfilled. He already knows that he has within himself powers not granted to everyone. He knows he has a gift of healing. He has already exercised it. He knows that he is able to command an audience, that people will listen to him. 'But if I really am the Messiah, Son of God in a special way, how is my ministry to be exercised?' So, the tempter says: 'If you are the Son of God, command these stones to become loaves of bread.'[35] He wonders whether he is to be an economic Messiah. Is he to get the people's attention by performing incredible feats? Should he seek earthly power and dominion? In fact, all these ways of proceeding are rejected and he begins his ministry, after the arrest of John the Baptist, making the very same announcement as the Baptist: 'Repent, for the kingdom of heaven has come near.'[36]

The scandal of Jesus' teaching

According to Matthew, there is continuity between the old and the new. 'The kingdom of God has come near . . . The kingdom of heaven is at hand.' Jesus told stories about the kingdom rooted in ordinary everyday experience, often containing an unexpected punch-line. 'The kingdom of God/the kingdom of heaven is like . . .' 'This is what it's like when God is in charge . . .' He presents a message that his hearers did not always find palatable. For example, there was his story about a landowner who went out early morning to hire labourers. Some started work after his first visit to the job-centre at six o'clock; he took more on at nine, twelve, three in the afternoon, and finally, an hour before knocking-off time, he took on some others who had been standing around all day. Yet when it came to paying them, he paid them all the same. Jesus had said at the beginning of the story that this is what it's like when God's in charge. 'The kingdom of heaven is like this.' The workers who had done a full day's work weren't happy to be paid the same as the rest, even though they received the sum they'd agreed, and the scandal of such an arrangement is clearly still felt 2,000 years later.

There are, however, instances in the gospels where the Church itself has become so familiar with the words of Jesus that they have lost their impact.

> Blessed are you who are poor, for yours is the kingdom of God.
> Blessed are you who are hungry now, for you will be filled.
> Blessed are you who weep now, for you will laugh.
> Blessed are you when people hate you, and when they exclude you, revile you, and defame you, on account of the Son of Man.
> Rejoice in that day and leap for joy, for surely your reward is great in heaven; for that is what their ancestors did to the prophets.
> But woe to you who are rich, for you have received your consolation.
> Woe to you who are full now, for you will be hungry.
> Woe to you who are laughing now, for you will mourn and weep.
> Woe to you when all speak well of you, for that is what their ancestors did to the false prophets.[37]

Of course such teaching may be dismissed as arrant, impractical nonsense simply on the grounds that that is not how we see the world today, especially when Jesus goes on to tell his hearers to love their enemies. In their first-century context there were, however, even more obvious grounds for being not just mildly bewildered by such silly teaching but openly hostile to something which runs contrary to the received wisdom of the Hebrew Scriptures. The very content of the Old Testament's vision of what it is to be blessed is shalom-peace. It consists in prosperity, wealth, many healthy children, especially sons, rich flocks of cattle, sheep and goats, plentiful harvest, all enjoyed under one's own vine and one's own fig-tree. Although in many places in the Psalms, and in particular in the Book of Job, this picture is challenged by the voice of the righteous sufferer, this is the prevailing understanding of true blessedness, absolute bliss, life lived out to a ripe old age in idyllic circumstances. Such abundance is always experienced as God's gift, his generosity lavished upon his people out of his gracious favour. In the case of Abram the promise came to include the gift of the land itself.[38]

Then Jesus came along and turned the Law and the Prophets upside down in a most scandalous way. 'Blessed are you who are poor, for yours is the kingdom of God.' Such words were deeply offensive to a people steeped in the Scriptures of the Old Testament. It's little wonder they dismissed him as mad and that what he said was considered blasphemous. Today's Church is so familiar with these words that even Christians have lost any sense of how offensive they are. The sign of blessedness, the sign that God is with his people, they have always been taught, is that they live to old age, prospering, growing wealthy, surrounded by their children. And in the face of that heritage Jesus says: 'Blessed are you who are poor . . . Blessed are you who are hungry now . . . Blessed are you who weep now . . .' Stuff and nonsense! But he doesn't even stop there. He adds insult to injury. 'Woe to you who are rich . . . Woe to you who are full now . . . Woe to you who are laughing now . . .' He turns their whole world upside down. What he says is subversive of the whole established order. He stands things on their head – which is not good news for those in power. Is it any wonder that they wanted to get rid of him as soon as possible? He was an affront to all established norms. They could see very clearly what a threat he was to them. Better get him out of the way in double quick time. It wasn't as if it were possible to separate the religious threat he constituted from his undermining of the secular basis of the community. They didn't make such a division anyway. As well as disturbing the people with his speeches, in his own person, by the way he acted with the penitent and the sick, he implicitly claimed the ability and the right to forgive people's sins. If that wasn't blasphemy, then what was!

In any case, what did it really mean to say that the poor are blessed, that the hungry are blessed, that those who mourn are blessed? In the Hebrew Scriptures, blessing is a sign of God's presence and favour. It shows that God has chosen the Jews for special treatment, that he is on their side. So, when Jesus says: 'Blessed are you who are poor . . .', he is making a similar claim on behalf of the dispossessed. The poor are blessed because God is with them. The hungry are blessed because God is with them. Mourners are blessed because God is with them. It is to them that in his goodness he shows his special favour. This is demonstrated not just in his words but in the very life of Jesus, who is heralded at the beginning of Matthew's Gospel, with the benefit of hindsight, as Emmanuel, God with us, God in it all with us.[39] The third evangelist, Luke, makes the link with Jesus' own person by describing the way Jesus understood himself and in the synagogue in Nazareth announced what he understood his life's work to be by quoting the prophet Isaiah. He claimed the prophecy for himself.

> The Spirit of the Lord is upon me, because he has anointed me to bring good news to the poor. He has sent me to proclaim release to the captives and recovery of sight to the blind, to let the oppressed go free, to proclaim the year of the Lord's favour.[40]

The claim made by the early Church was that in Jesus God demonstrated that he is with everyone, even those whom the Jewish people have marginalised. Mary, the mother of Jesus, praises God because he has come to the aid of the deprived and the dispossessed:

> He has shown strength with his arm; he has scattered the proud in the thoughts of their hearts. He has brought down the powerful from their thrones, and lifted up the lowly; he has filled the hungry with good things, and sent the rich away empty.[41]

Jesus was suckled on Mary's upside-down, back-to-front thinking. The poor are blessed because God is on their side.

This Jesus of Nazareth did not, however, repudiate the Jewish scriptures. He claimed to fulfil them; he filled them with fuller meaning. There was indeed continuity between the old and the new. He knew that God wants everything he has made to flourish and prosper, as the Hebrew Scriptures make clear. He knew that it is God's will that everyone should be happy. He showed a healthy enjoyment of life at many a party. He was no killjoy. He had none the less an overwhelming sense of God's righteousness, which led him to show partiality to the poor, the hungry and the oppressed, to those deprived of their share of his lavish provision. The rich and the wealthy were keeping the good gifts of God's plenty to themselves. They had forgotten that blessing always comes as his gift and that it is given for the sake of all. Jesus was saddened when a rich young aristocrat came to him with profound questions. Jesus told him that if he wanted to be perfect, to go, sell his possessions, and give the money to the poor, and he would have treasure in heaven. Then he would be able to follow with the other disciples. He couldn't do it.[42] The wealth God had given him was in trust for others, but he could not let go. His possessions had taken possession of him and Jesus wistfully observed how hard it would be for a rich person to enter the kingdom of heaven.

> Again I tell you, it is easier for a camel to go through the eye of a needle than for someone who is rich to enter the kingdom of God.

Therein lay the scandal as the disciples were quick to see. 'Then who can be saved?' If the rich – who are rich because they have been blessed by God – cannot enter easily into the kingdom of heaven, what chance has anyone else? What Jesus was saying went against everything they had been taught. One might well expect the scribes, the teachers of the Law to get upset! But the disciples themselves, with all the advantages of being with him constantly, are portrayed as equally uncomprehending, or at best as understanding in moments of insight and then losing hold almost immediately on what they have seen.

Caesarea Philippi[43]

When this man, Jesus of Nazareth, approached them whilst at work mending their nets, they followed and they rapidly discovered that this was no ordinary person. His teaching was strangely compelling and his gift of healing was demonstrated time and time again. It wasn't difficult to attract a crowd in such circumstances. Word soon went round that he was in the neighbourhood and people gathered from every corner to hear him speak and to seek remedy for their ills. He was very special. The whole of the initial period of Jesus' ministry has nevertheless an exploratory feel about it. Jesus is exercising publicly his gifts of preaching, teaching and healing, but is he really the one they have been taught to expect? At Caesarea Philippi Jesus puts what many commentators treat as a test question, as if Jesus himself knows the answer: 'Who do people say that the Son of Man is?' Jesus may perhaps be seeking corroboration of what he himself has come to believe to be the case. He is certainly interested in what others have to say and specifically what his disciples think. They themselves have heard all kinds of opinions. John the Baptist? Elijah? Jeremiah or others of the prophets? In themselves such identifications are remarkable. It is no commonplace to believe that he is one of the prophets restored to the present world. 'But who do you say that I am?' Jesus persists. Simon Peter answered, 'You are the Messiah [or the Christ], the Son of the living God.'[44] And it must be a matter of debate as to whether, at this juncture in the story, the S of 'Son' is upper or lower case. In a flash of insight Peter moves beyond the simple knowledge that this Jesus of Nazareth is a very special human being to the assertion that this is the Messiah, the Christ, the Anointed One, specially chosen of God to lead his people. There had been, and would yet be, other claimants to the title. There was a general expectation that God would send a deliverer, but that did not of itself mean that the one who was recognised to be the Messiah was necessarily divine. He would be a human being writ large, no ordinary person. The tendency over the years has been to stress the divinity rather than emphasise his humanity, but at this stage on the journey to acknowledge Jesus as the Christ is to live within the expectations of the Jewish people. As for the attribution of the title 'Son of the living God', there are no capital letters in the Greek text. So the translator takes a critical decision by writing 'son' or 'Son'. Whatever is written 'S/son of the living God' bears a strong sense of Jesus' special relationship with the God of Israel, but if the capital S is used a further measure of interpretation has taken place and the assessment of who Jesus is has moved a notch further towards the divine. Jesus congratulates Simon Peter on this flash of insight. However, the congratulations soon move to reproach.

It was not merely Jesus' teaching that caused offence. He himself was an offence to everything for which they hoped. The expectation that the Messiah would be an anointed king and deliverer was an accepted part of contemporary Jewish belief. There were many claimants to be Messiah. But, having extracted from Simon Peter and the other disciples the confession that he is God's anointed one, Jesus commanded the disciples not to tell anyone about it. Certainly as things were to develop he could not expect people to believe it.

> From that time on, Jesus began to show his disciples that he must go to Jerusalem and undergo great suffering at the hands of the elders and chief priests and scribes, and be killed, and on the third day be raised.[45]

This was more than Peter could stomach. 'God forbid,' he said, and immediately received Jesus' rebuke:

> Get behind me, Satan! You are a stumbling block to me; for you are setting your mind not on divine things but on human things.

Jesus could see that just as the prophets had been persecuted, so he could expect no less. None the less from the perspective of the disciples travelling with him, without the wonderful gift of hindsight which was later to illuminate what had happened, the idea that the Messiah would suffer was a very difficult concept to accept. Was this really how it was to be? Did he really mean it when he said that those who wanted to be his disciples must take up their cross too?

Transfiguration[46]

If Jesus' baptism at the hands of John is to be understood in terms of his apprehension of his special relationship with God and the awareness that he is to have a special ministry, then the transfiguration is his confirmation that the way on which he has embarked and that his understanding of the way he is to proceed is the right path. 'This is my Son, the Beloved; with him I am well pleased . . .'[47] The words reported at the baptism are repeated on the mountain top in the presence of the inner wheel of disciples, Peter, James and John. This time it is not just a matter of Jesus' self-questioning. It is also a point of disclosure for the three disciples. They hear the voice from the cloud, affirming that this is my Son, the Beloved; with him I am well pleased, and additionally they are told to 'listen to him'[48].

The ensuing conversation is about the Jewish expectation that Elijah will come before God's final reign is inaugurated, a hope that is still alive at the Passover celebration when a place is left empty for Elijah. In fact, Jesus expresses the belief that Elijah has already come in the person of John the Baptist. The scribes did not recognise him. They got him out of the way because he was an embarrassment to Herod. Jesus clearly expects that they will treat him in the same way and that he too will suffer at their hands.

However, the story of the transfiguration itself contains, as an integral part, an account of the coming of Elijah together with Moses. Jesus is confirmed in his belief that he has a special relationship with God and a special mission from God, being presented as the fufilment of the Law and the Prophets. He is declared to be the one to whom the Law and the prophets point. Moses and Elijah confer with him and the disciples recognise him in all his glory. This is affirmation for Jesus. He is on the right track, but this is for the disciples too a confirming experience. In 2 Peter we are reminded that they were there:

> For we did not follow cleverly devised myths when we made known to you the power and coming of our Lord Jesus Christ, but we had been eyewitnesses of his majesty. For he received honour and glory from God the Father when that voice was conveyed to him by the Majestic Glory, saying, 'This is my Son, my Beloved, with whom I am well pleased.' We ourselves heard this voice come from heaven, while we were with him on the holy mountain.[49]

As a boy I used to travel on the same bus day after day the three miles to school. It cost three-halfpence (in old money). Because the bus conductors were not infinite in number and because their schedules meant that they each had a turn on the 185 we got to recognise them. One particular man had a baggy uniform which didn't touch him in many places. We made his life a misery. He must have dreaded the time of day when we were going to school. We used to take the middle out of those early messy biros, roll pellets of paper, or occasionally use rice, to make a peashooter and fire at him as he went down the central aisle collecting fares. It is a wonder that he himself did not take positive action against us.

Anyway, one day we were marched in twos, with caps and blazers, from school to the Town Hall, where we were ushered into the Council Chamber, with its panelled walls with the name of the town's worthies in gold letters. We sat on the padded benches which wheezed as we lowered ourselves onto them. We were as subdued as if in a cathedral. Then the high double doors opened and in came a strangely dressed man solemnly carrying a large, heavy, gold mace which he ceremomiously placed on the polished bench in front of the central high-backed carved chair in front of us. Behind him came the Mayor in a splendid scarlet cloak with a gold chain, from which dangled a heavy enamelled badge bearing the town's coat of arms. He wore a black tricorn hat and a white lace frilled ruff. What an amazing figure! It was our scruffy bus conductor! The funny thing is that we never again fired our peashooters at him. Although on the bus he continued to have a very loose relationship with his clothing we had seen him resplendent in his mayoral garb. We had seen him in all his glory.

Peter, James and John did not forget the moment of insight when briefly they grasped who this Jesus of Nazareth was and what he was about. In common with many for whom the penny drops they wanted to try and hold on to the experience. Peter wanted to build booths to mark the spot but had to be content to remember the vision. Jesus again required the disciples to keep quiet about it.

> Tell no one about the vision until after the Son of Man has been raised from the dead.[50]

The approaching end

The secret was to be kept until the Son of Man has been raised from the dead. Jesus' self-designation as the Son of man – for such would seem to be the way in which somewhat enigmatically Jesus talked about himself – is a term embedded in apocalyptic literature to describe a figure of power who would come from God.

> I saw one like a human being[51] coming with
> The clouds of heaven.
> And he came to the Ancient One and was
> presented before him.
> To him was given dominion and glory and
> kingship, that all peoples, nations, and
> languages should serve him.
> His dominion is an everlasting dominion that
> shall not pass away,
> And his kingship is one that shall never be
> destroyed.

A great deal of scholarly ink has been spilled discussing the significance of the phrase 'Son of Man'. The words are here written upper case because although this expression clearly refers to a figure in human shape this is a very special human being. He is given all the attributes of kingship and is no ordinary mortal. Yet this Son of Man coming from God, filled with divine power, is not yet God *tout court*. It is indeed in the conversation with his disciples at Caesarea Philippi that, as Matthew presents it, the realisation of the special status of Jesus is advanced. Both his self-understanding and the growing awareness within the disciples of who he is move a notch on the scale between human and divine. 'Who do people say the Son of Man is?' and '. . . who do you say that I am?' are set in parallel. It would be a perfectly proper question to ask: 'Who do people say the Son of Man is?' and mean: 'Who do people believe this special human being to be?' In fact, the answers given 'John the Baptist, Elijah, Jeremiah or one of the other prophets' suggest such an understanding, which does not necessarily equate the Son of Man with Jesus. However, when Jesus in the wake of these reports, asks: 'Who do you say that I am?' the parallelism of the two questions provokes Peter's reply: 'You are the Messiah, the Son of the living God.' Clearly in Matthew's view of the event the son of man, the human being endowed with power from God, with all the trappings of kingship, is one and the same Messiah/Christ, God's promised anointed King, not merely human but son of God in a special sense. Yet having come to this tremendous conclusion, and even after the transfiguration confirming Jesus' awesome sense of calling to be the fulfilment of the Law and the Prophets, the disciples are still enjoined to keep silent, not to tell anyone that he is the Christ, because the power of the Son of man, the power of the anointed King is to be redefined in terms of suffering, death and resurrection.

What a funny way of being God!

The concept of power with which people operate today is not noticeably different from the way in which the disciples understood it 2000 years ago. Status is about acquiring a position of pre-eminence. Authority and power are about the ability to get things done, whether by persuasion or coercion does not really matter as long as the desired outcome is achieved. One of the greatest stumbling blocks to faith in God is the fact that he is conceived of as having power which he fails to use to put right the things which in human terms need a solution. Surely if he is love as Christians claim then he should use his power to overcome evil and put an end to disease and suffering. But then we are getting ahead of our story, for that does not appear to be God's way of being God, if he is indeed to be known through Jesus.

In his lifetime on many occasions Jesus of Nazareth insisted that the way to true greatness is through service and candidates for entry into the kingdom of heaven must become childlike. His disciples wanted to know who is the greatest in the kingdom. His response is to take a little child and say:

> Truly I tell you, unless you change and become like children, you will never enter the kingdom of heaven. Whoever becomes humble like this child is the greatest in the kingdom of heaven. Whoever welcomes one such child in my name welcomes me.[52]

When the mother of James and John came to ask a favour, she asked him to let her two sons sit one on his right hand and the other on his left when he comes into his kingdom. These would be the positions of greatest influence, to be next to him to offer counsel. Jesus' response is to ask if they are 'able to drink the cup which I am about to drink?'[53] Will they accept a path that leads to suffering and death? They think they can. They do not yet know that that will be the way they will indeed have to go. But position and status do not belong to Jesus. They are his Father's, to give to whom he will. Jesus once again emphasises the upside-down nature of his message.

> You know that the rulers of the Gentiles lord it over them, and their great ones are tyrants over them. It will not be so among you; but whoever wishes to be great among you must be your servant, and whoever wishes to be first among you must be your slave; just as the Son of Man came not to be served but to serve, and to give his life a ransom for many.[54]

The scandal of what Jesus had to say was felt acutely. Right up to the end his message was not properly heard. On the night before he died, the evangelist John tells how, at supper, he took a towel and washed his disciples' feet. Jesus lived his topsy-turvy message by being a servant to his friends – not really the act of a king.[55] At the moment of his arrest Simon Peter produced a sword in an attempt to prevent Jesus being taken and proceeded to cut off the ear of the High Priest's slave Malchus. Jesus healed the man and told Peter to put up his sword. This is not the way. 'Am I not to drink the cup that the Father has given me?'[56] This is what he has been talking about, the inevitablity of misunderstanding, rejection, suffering and death. He did not want to die but in Gethsemane, in spite of his tortured prayer, 'Let this cup pass from me', he knows that there is no way out. 'My Father, if this cannot pass unless I drink it, your will be done.'[57] The travesty of a trial, the scourging, the mockery, the death penalty of a common felon – he was not much of a king with his purple cloak and crown of thorns. There were no battalions of angels to come to his rescue. He had to drink the cup to the bitter dregs – to the point where he felt utterly abandoned by the God he had called Father. If this was God nailed to a cross on a hill outside Jerusalem, it was a strange way of showing it! This did not look much like success. If it was success, Jesus in his living and dying must have redefined what it means to be powerful and strong.

Our contemporary world seems to think that real power is the ability to make things happen, power of the snap-your-fingers type. Jesus proclaims in his life and death that power is the power of service expressed in love of God and of our neighbour. This is expressed in a very striking fashion by the Japanese Christian writer Shusaku Endo.[58]

Rodrigues is a priest living in 17th century Japan. He is a contemplative by temperament and spends hours in meditation before the figure of Christ on his cross. He has no visions and he hears no voices. Like many of his contemporaries he lives with the constant fear of arrest and the possibility of torture because of his faith. He is determined that he will stand firm. He will be strong, and as far as he himself is concerned, when he is subsequently arrested, that is what happens. He is routinely imprisoned. He can continue in his cell his meditation of Christ on his cross. No matter what the threat to himself he will trust in God to sustain him. But he is then told that what he had thought was the snoring of the guards in the next room is in fact the groans of Christians hanging by their feet over pits of excrement. Their torment will continue until he renounces his God. All he has to do to signify that he has turned away from Christ is to grind his foot on a 'fumie', a crucifix on the floor in front of him.

> The first rays of the dawn appear. The light shines on his long neck stretched out like a chicken and upon the bony shoulders. The priest grasps the fumie with both hands bringing it close to his eyes. He would like to press to his own face that face trampled on by so many feet. With saddened glance he stares intently at the man in the centre of the fumie, worn down and hollow with the constant trampling. A tear is about to fall from his eye. 'Ah,' he says trembling, 'the pain!'
>
> 'It is only a formality. What do formalities matter?' The interpreter urges him on excitedly. 'Only go through with the exterior form of trampling.'
>
> The priest raises his foot. In it he feels a dull, heavy pain. This is no mere formality. He will now trample on what he has considered the most beautiful thing in his life, on what he has believed most pure, on what is filled with the ideals and the dreams of man. How his foot aches! And then the Christ in bronze speaks to the priest: 'Trample! Trample! I more than anyone know of the pain in your foot. Trample! It was to be trampled on by men that I was born into this world. It was to share men's pain that I carried my cross.'
>
> The priest placed his foot on the fumie. Dawn broke. And far in the distance the cock crew.

The echo of Peter's denial of Jesus in the High Priest's courtyard is unmistakable. Yet perhaps the action of the priest in denying his God for the sake of the suffering people in the neighbouring cell, at the risk of his own soul, is more Christ-like than any stubborn display of strength which keeps his integrity intact and leaves his brothers and sisters to suffer. Notice also that Rodrigues, for the first time in his life, heard God speak. The silence of God was broken.

If death on the hill of Calvary was the outcome of Jesus' special mission, his calling as God's Messiah, just what had he achieved? In the eyes even of his disciples the cross looked like the end of everything. If that *had* been the end, it is not likely that this Jesus would have been remembered, except perhaps as a comma in a sentence in a history book, a passing memory of a preacher who had some pretty wild things to say. He might just have been remembered as a healer who like others before and after him had a gift which brought relief to the pain and suffering of some of his contemporaries. Yet even in his death this man from Nazareth is reported as making an impression even on the rough soldiery that led him to his death. 'Truly this man was God's Son [or: a son of God],'[59] the words attributed to the Roman centurion at the foot of the cross, mark him out as someone who had been a very special human being, but not yet the Second Person of the Trinity[60], as in Matthew's Gospel, nor yet with Thomas in John's Gospel, 'My Lord and my God!'[61] Jesus died and his disciples, who had begun to place high expectations in him, fled. It is the announcement of his resurrection that makes the difference.

4

RESURRECTION

If anything is the heart of the matter, this is. It is the belief that on the third day after the crucifixion, *God raised Jesus from the dead.* Note the passive form of the expression, which is, I believe, infinitely preferable to saying that Jesus rose from the dead. Jesus did not have some kind of out-of-body experience, seeing his own dead body on the cross and deciding to rise from the dead. That does not, it seems to me, take death seriously. Jesus was not in a swoon nor did he walk automatically through a doorway into everlasting life. He was dead, end, full-stop. It was by the active agency of God that he was raised from death. This was not the movement of a soul from its bodily imprisonment to a realm which naturally belongs to it. There was nothing automatic about it. Jesus was dead.

The disciples were right to feel bereft. They could hardly be blamed for feeling that this was the end of all their hopes. The next step belonged to God and to God alone, for he is the only one who can raise the dead. On the third day after the crucifixion, Christians believe, God did act decisively. He raised Jesus from the dead. If the incarnation, God's decision to take human flesh and live amongst us, is in the time sequence of the Christian story the first critical act of God, the resurrection is the pivotal act without which the incarnation would never have been noticed. The resurrection is the central act of God without which none of the rest would have been possible.

We read everything that went before in the light of the resurrection. It is the resurrection which enables the Church to talk about the cross of Christ as a sacrifice made on behalf of the human race for the remission of sin. This interpretation laid over the story of the shameful death of Jesus of Nazareth is only possible because of the prior belief that God raised him from the dead. None of the development of doctrine that took place over decades would have happened if the early Church had not felt obliged, in the light of the resurrection, to tease out the consequences of believing that Jesus is the Christ and Son of the living God. We read what happened after Easter Day in the light of the focal belief that Christ is alive and that he is still to be experienced through the presence of the Holy Spirit. If there was no resurrection then our faith is vain, as Paul says categorically:

> . . . if Christ has not been raised, then our proclamation has been vain and your faith has been in vain.
>
> 1 Corinthians 15:14

and

> If Christ has not been raised, your faith is futile and you are still in your sins.
>
> 1 Corinthians 15:17

In fact 1 Corinthians 15 is a critical passage for any discussion of resurrection, being the earliest testimony we have of events which Paul himself had received. He himself is not the origin of the list of appearances. He is simply handing on the tradition that has been handed on to him. What is sure is that the claim that God has raised Jesus from the dead is at the very heart of Christian belief. Without it the rest comes tumbling down like a house of cards.

One noticeable thing in Paul's lists of appearances of the risen Christ to Peter and the Twelve, to 500 disciples at one time, to James and then to Paul himself, is that there is no mention of an empty tomb. There is no doubt that the testimony of scripture is that the tomb was empty but if the testimony of the early Church is to be accepted the primary experience and belief was that Christ is alive. My own basic experience was nothing to do with whether the tomb was empty. I have subsequently come to believe that the balance of probability is that it was empty, but the plank on which my faith rests is not the belief that the Body of Christ had disappeared from the place where it was buried. I believe that he is alive and active in the world today. I believe that I met the risen Christ in the body of faithful believers, the Body of Christ, amongst whom I worshipped week by week. I met him through the preaching which itself was rooted in the biblical witness. I have subsequently met him in worship 'where two or three are gathered together' for he promised to be there. I have met him in the celebration of Holy Communion, where as host at the meal he says: 'This is my body.' I have met him in those in need whom I have been able to serve. I have met him in those who have served me. This is my faith, which I believe is also the faith of the Church. I have written repeatedly, 'I believe . . .' I have proved nothing. Yet starting from the central point of belief, that Christ is alive, and wrestling with the consequences of believing it, I remain convinced that the dying-rising way of life of Jesus is the best clue we have to the way in which life should be lived.

To begin with the tomb and to try and demonstrate that Christ must be risen because there is no better explanation of why the tomb was empty seems to me, in the order of experience, the wrong way. It is the conviction that Christ is alive, that God has raised him from the dead which is the primary experience. In consequence, believers in retrospect believe that the tomb must have been empty. Discussions about who moved the stone may help to demonstrate that some of the possible explanations are more difficult to believe than the straight belief that raising Jesus was the work of God, but they prove nothing. Preachers still have to invite their hearers to bet their lives on the belief that Christ is alive and well. They still have to invite them to worship the God made known through this Jesus in the certainty that this belief will provide meaning and direction to their lives. In short, following this Lord will make coherent sense of life. The thing that makes this possible is the knowledge that God raised him from the dead and that we live in his presence.

Doctrine and the Liturgical Year

I have suggested that it is both profitable and desirable that we should get inside the story of Jesus of Nazareth by walking alongside the first disciples. This will help us understand how incredible claims came to be made about this man to the point where the Church recognised in him 'My Lord and my God!' We ought then to appreciate that the developed doctrine of the Church was not the whimsical fabrication of a group of people who in the process of inventing a new religion found themselves at the centre of things. It was not something that they wilfully brought about out of self-interest. It was something that they felt impelled to do. It was in fact much against the character of these first believers to focus any attention on themselves. It was about Jesus that they felt compelled to speak. It was not of their choosing but a necessary process of reflection. They felt driven to accept the logic of what they had experienced.

If this Jesus was indeed the Messiah and son of the living God, if he had been raised again, as they believed, if this was in fact their Lord and God, then all kinds of things seemed to follow. They needed to be worked through. How could this carpenter from Nazareth be God? How can God become human? If he is God then he must always have been there. There was no point when he was not. He must have been pre-existent and involved in creation. If their experience of the Holy Spirit was real how was the Spirit linked to the Father and the Son? God is one, yet they had experienced him in three ways. So the doctrine of the Trinity which had already been set down as a formula at the end of Matthew's Gospel had to be worked through to tease out the logic of what was being claimed. In the light of the resurrection this doctrinal development had to take place. The outcome was the formulation of the Creeds which were the Church's attempt to extract from the story those things which Christian faith requires.

One way in which Christians today can be helped to take hold of the fundamental questions with which thinking people have to grapple is to celebrate the life of Christ through the drama of the Liturgical Year. Not every inquirer asks complicated questions, but even the most unsophisticated will wonder how Jesus could be both God and a human being at the same time. Most will wonder whether the doctrine of the Trinity is strictly necessary. To some at least it will seem unnecessarily convoluted. Every seeker deserves some help in this direction and it is the task of the preacher to show in story form how the first disciples felt themselves pushed by their experience to conclusions that no one would have wanted to invent. One way of doing this is walk with them through the life of Christ. The order which is imposed by the Church's Year may not be entirely satisfactory but it does give a framework to what might otherwise be random, pepper-pot preaching. It is, I hope, inconceivable that anyone should preach on anything other than the resurrection on Easter Day, although many preachers do seem to find Trinity Sunday a convenient time to take their annual holidays!

Advent and the promise of Christmas

Usually considered to be the beginning of the Christian year Advent is the bridge between the old and the new. Christian origins are plainly identified within the context of Jewish expectation. The Christian religion does not spring like water from the rock but is in continuity with what has gone before. The Jews looked forward, as they still do, to the coming of the Messiah, the Christ, the anointed king of Israel. Christians find in Jesus of Nazareth the fulfilment of God's promise of deliverance, although the outcome is in many respects different from Jewish hope. Jesus the Messiah, whose very name means Saviour, was not a sword-carrying warrior. He was a man of peace. His lordship was not about dominance, but about servanthood. Above all he was to die the death of a common criminal, which in Jewish understanding debarred him from being the Coming One. The Jewish Messiah could not be executed in such a shameful way. There is severe disjuncture but there is no doubt either of the continuity. Jesus knew the Jewish Scriptures and found there categories in which to understand his own mission. The early Church too spoke of him as the one who had come to fulfil prophecy. In the light of their experience of Jesus they were able to put a new spin on what they had been taught to believe.

One of the key words in speaking of God's expected intervention in the affairs of Israel is the word *preparation*. The pivotal character between the old and the new is John the Baptist who is described as the forerunner of the Messiah. He too is the fulfilment of prophecy. He came to prepare the way of the Lord (see Isaiah 40:3-5). He is also identified with the return of the prophet Elijah[62] who was to come before the appearance of the Messiah. His job is to point to Jesus, to arouse the people's expectation of the imminent arrival of one whose shoes he was not worthy to unfasten. He was not himself part of the new era that was about to dawn. His task was to be the signpost.

The other key figures in the preparation for the arrival of God's deliverer are Mary and Joseph. Although Joseph is given an angelic visitation his role is limited to accepting that what is about to happen is of God. He is not to be afraid of taking Mary as his wife (Matthew 1:20) and the child to be born is to be called Jesus. Although the genealogy of the Messiah is traced through Joseph (of which more below), in Advent the traditional focus in the Church's liturgy has been Mary. In the Protestant tradition preachers have often been wary of speaking about her because of what they believe to be unwarranted claims made for her by the Roman Catholic and Orthodox. They do, however, have to beware of throwing out the mother with the bath water. They may draw back from speaking of her as Queen of Heaven. They may not want to preach about her immaculate conception, her perpetual virginity or her bodily assumption into heaven.

Nevertheless, she might, in her obedience to God, be properly described as the Mother of the Church and there can be no reason whatsoever for failing to honour her as the mother of Jesus of Nazareth whom the Church came to believe is the Son of God. The words of the Magnificat which are attributed to Mary, with its overturning of the social order, foreshadow the upside-down teaching of her son. Her formative influence on him must have been immense and for that reason alone she deserves to be honoured.

The fourth traditional strand of the preparatory season of Advent relates to our long-term vision. Advent is itself preparation for the birth of the Christ-child at Christmas but at the same time it points us beyond the life, death and resurrection of Jesus to the completion of all things with his Second Coming, sometimes referred to as the Parousia. This is an area which abounds with exotic apocalyptic imagery which has often proved a valuable quarry for all sorts of crackpots. Speculation about when the Second Coming will be, and the manner of it, should be avoided. The imagery belongs to a cultural setting which no longer pertains. That does not, however, mean that we can dispense with the idea of an End-Time altogether. If the religious quest is indeed about finding meaning and direction in life the story we tell needs to be going somewhere. As to the imagery describing that time I believe that this is an area where we may be reverently agnostic. We do not need to speculate about the furniture of heaven or draw the plans of the City of God. We ought to be content to believe that life in the nearer presence of God will be infinitely more wonderful than anything we can conceive and leave the rest to him.

The Advent season is rich in themes for the Christian preacher. Through the stories and the traditional passages of scripture which are available to us they can be opened up to a world, and indeed Church congregations, which must hear them afresh. Above all they ought to be helped to look forward with hope.

Incarnation – the birth of Christ

If we are going to preach that God took our flesh and was born in a scrap of humanity, a tiny baby, in a stable in Bethlehem the first thing we have to do is recover our sense of wonder. It has become such a commonplace claim that even worshipping, practising Christians have forgotten what an amazing statement it is. We are saying that the God who is greater than everything that exists, who upholds the universe by his will and power, the God who is holy, 'high and lifted up' became a frail human baby in an obscure place in the Middle East. All of this stems from the belief that Jesus of Nazareth was truly God and truly human. The God of the Hebrew Scriptures is beyond the world, greater than our conceiving. He is a mysterious hidden God unless he decides to reveal himself to us by an act of will or grace. Yet Christians have the audacity to believe that Jesus of Nazareth is the image of the invisible God. We need to recapture a sense of what a stupendous affirmation that is.

> To conceive of God as simply infinite mystery, as the Void beyond our conceiving, was to lapse into silence. It was to say too little. To conceive of God as simply presence, as mercy, as friend, as ally, was to risk . . . a reduction of the mystery to the level of easy familiarity. It was to say more than should be said.[63]

We have so domesticated God that we no longer appreciate that at the very heart of our faith is the paradox that the transcendent, holy God became a real human being like you and me.

It is, of course, the nature of paradox that two complementary things are asserted neither of which can be surrendered. Jesus was fully God. Jesus was fully human. Both sides of the paradox are held to be true. Neither statement is to be denied or reduced in meaning. Jesus Christ was God in every way that God is God. Jesus Christ was human in the same way every human being is human. This paradox was chewed over for the best part of four centuries and at the end of that time the two things are asserted alongside each other. He is

> God from God, Light from Light, true God from true God . . . he came down from heaven, was incarnate of the Holy Spirit and the Virgin Mary and became truly human . . .

Neither is modified nor watered down in the light of the other. After decades of dispute the Church was no further down the road than it was when the beginning of the Gospels of Matthew and Luke were written. They both contain stories about the birth of Jesus in Bethlehem from the Virgin Mary alongside long lists of names which are specifically there to link Jesus of Nazareth to the House of David, for it was from there that in Jewish expectation the Messiah was to come. The genealogies are as necessary a part of the paradox as are accounts of Jesus' birth through a Virgin.

The tendency, however, in spite of the professed need to hold onto both parts of the paradox has been in the course of the history of doctrine to divinise rather than to heighten the humanity. There has often been the temptation when asked how the human Jesus could possibly do this or that, to say: 'Well, he could do it because he was God.' That seems to me an unacceptable blurring of the two sides of the paradox. What every preacher should keep in mind is the difference it makes whether one begins *above* with God or *below* with human beings in making assertions about what is or is not possible. However, although God may be omnipresent, Jesus certainly was not. Although God may be all-powerful Jesus most certainly was not. Although God may know everything that is knowable, Jesus himself disavowed foreknowledge of times and places which are known only to the Father. Furthermore, if we begin *above* with God and think about how God could become a human being with all the limitations involved in being human, then there must be some element of what is called *kenosis,* God's *self*-emptying or *self*-limitation, in order for any conjunction of divinity and humanity to be possible.

God must have accepted voluntarily limits on his power and knowledge in the human Jesus. Certainly the Christian preacher needs to be aware of the difference it makes in choosing a starting point in any talk about the being and activity of God in Jesus Christ.

In terms of God's being Christology *from above* must take priority. Functionally, in terms of our salvation, Christology *from below* must take priority. The great Reformation dictum was. 'To know Christ is to know his benefits.' But in terms of logic *who Jesus is* must come before our experience of him as Saviour. He does not and cannot become God and Human Being because he saves us. He saves us because he is both God and Human Being. Teaching about his Person precedes our experience of him as Redeemer.

The debate about the Person of Christ will to many seem overly complicated. None the less we are obliged to wrestle with the paradox. The orthodox conclusion was that Jesus Christ is 'one person in two natures'. At the Council of Chalcedon certain heretical options were excluded in a formal statement, which said:

> One and the same Christ, Son, Lord, Only-begotten, recognised in two natures, without confusion, without change, without division, without separation, the distinction of natures being in no way annulled by the union, but rather the characteristics of each nature being preserved and coming together to form one person.

These stipulations became the goalposts between which play must take place. However, it is clear that stories are much more likely to communicate than such dogmatic statements. None the less, as responsible storytellers we must check out our stories to determine whether they are on the pitch or have in fact strayed beyond the carefully defined area which the Church has used over the centuries. It will not do to dismiss the whole debate by saying that it is a mystery, that is, 'I am not prepared to think about it.' There is, however, a proper sense in which the heart of the gospel centres on a true mystery, namely that the holy and invisible God should deign to take real human flesh and speak to us from the inside. This astounding paradox is best felt and understood in worship which acknowledges both God's majesty and yet celebrates his presence with us.

The saving work of Christ

Whereas the Church laid down very carefully the parameters within which discussion of the person of Christ is possible, it has never pronounced any particular theory about the work of Christ to be required of Christian believers. In fact, although theories of the atonement abound none was given the official imprimatur of the Ecumenical Councils. Those that survive to the present day in one shape or another have some rootage in the Scriptures, but to describe the work of Christ on the cross simply in terms of atonement seems to me less than adequate since I believe that what happened on the cross is as much about suffering as it is about overcoming sin. However, even though no formal definition of Christ's saving work is laid down as required of the believer, that does not mean that we can hold any view we like. There are some very basic ground rules for talking about the cross. For example, (i) has the theory offered any grounding in the Bible? (ii) What does the theory say about God? Does it offer a worthy picture of him? (iii) How culturally conditioned is it? Would what is offered be understood anywhere and at any time? Furthermore, there are two movements in making viable any understanding of what Christ achieved on the cross. There has to be first and foremost a description of what objectively was achieved by Christ's death, and secondly, something needs to be said about how what was done on Calvary benefited human beings. So, a rapid survey of the attempts to describe the work of Christ.

A. Christus Victor, the classic/dramatic theory

Associated since 1930 with the name of Gustaf Aulén Christ's work is spoken of in terms of victory, a battle won against the powers which are hostile to humanity, namely, sin, death and the devil. They were defeated. (For the defeat of sin cf. Matthew 4 and Luke 4, Mark 14:36 and parallels; Phillipians 2:8; Hebrews 5:7-8. For the defeat of death cf. 1 Corinthians 15:45-46; 2 Timothy 1:10. For the defeat of the devil cf. Mark 3:22; Colossians 2:15; John 12:31; Hebrews 2:14-15; 1 John 3:8 et al. Human beings are freed from the powers that hold them prisoner. They have shown themselves incapable of defeating evil by their own powers. Only God can deliver us, but because it had to be within the conditions of humanity that victory was won, Christ had to be truly human. Because he was truly human it is possible for others to share his victory cf. 1 Corinthians 15:57 where God gives us the victory, and Romans 8:37 where we are more than conquerors through him who loved us).

This theory offers strong imagery which strikes chords deep within us and it manifestly treats the forces of evil with the utmost seriousness. On the other hand it presents a highly mythologised picture. It risks making God and the Devil opponents in a dualistic fashion. But the most serious question with which it leaves us is just what sort of victory was won? Have the powers of evil really been defeated? How do we explain the continuing evidence for the presence and practice of evil in everyday life 2000 years on?

B. Reparation Theories

(a) Theories of sacrifice

The various ways in which God's activity on the Cross is spoken of as 'sacrifice' are built on the notion that there has been a break in relationship caused by human beings which requires sacrifice to repair the damaged relationship. In biblical terms the Letter to the Hebrews is the place where the work of Christ is elaborated against the background of Old Testament sacrifice. There Christ offers himself to the Father as the sacrificial victim and God accepts the sacrifice once and for all (cf. also Romans 3:25; 8:3).

In the most acceptable kind of sacrificial understanding of Christ's achievement on the cross it is God himself who provides the sacrifice (cf. Leviticus 17:11 and the story of the sacrifice of Isaac at the hands of his father Abraham). However, pictures of sacrifice can so easily present an ethically unacceptable vision of God. It can all too easily look as if there is a rift in the Godhead where the Father has to be placated by the Son. This kind of view of the cross can really only be helpful if the imagery is given a strong ethical content, making it clear that there are matters of justice and judgement at stake. Sacrifice can so easily become manipulation and leave us with an impossible picture of an immoral God.

(b) The Satisfaction Theory

St Anselm was an 11th century Archbishop of Canterbury who published in 1097 *Cur Deus Homo:* Why did God become man? or Why God became (hu)man. Human sin, it is claimed, has sullied God's honour. God can forgive that offence if he receives adequate compensation or, to use the mediaeval chivalrous word, 'satisfaction'. Sin is serious because it is against God. No human being is capable of making the reparation required. Our sin is infinitely grievous precisely because it is against God. No one, therefore, can make satisfaction except God. So, God became human in order that satisfaction might be made. Now, Jesus Christ who offered himself was innocent of any sin. Therefore God contracted a debt towards him. Since he himself lacked nothing, the reward of his merits are transferred to the rest of humankind in terms of the remission of our sins. As well as sharing the common problem of reparation theories that they point to an unhealthy split in the Godhead between a blameless Son and a Father who has to be made sweet, Anselm's Satisfaction Theory is heavily culturally conditioned. We do not live in a world of knights in shining armour, where kings have champions to defend their sullied honour.

This view of the cross is of interest if we have a picture of *Ivanhoe* in our mind's eye!

(c) Punitive Theories

These theories are usually predicated on the belief that to safeguard God's righteousness, sin cannot be permitted. The justice of God requires that sin be punished. The sins of humankind are transferred to Christ who underwent the punishment that our sin deserves, which leaves us with a real problem, driving a wedge between the Father and the Son, making a 'goodie' out of the Son and a 'baddie' out of the Father! The only way out of that, it seems to me, is to insist on the Father's own suffering in giving up his only Son to punishment, pain, suffering and death.

Reparation theories as a whole do take human sin seriously. It is not shrugged off as of little or no consequence. They take account of the holiness of God to whom sin is totally abhorrent but even here severe objections could be lodged against a just God punishing an innocent human being. How the transfer of merits works is difficult to grasp and communicate. The various versions of Reparation theory all involve the notion of the transfer of merit in one way or another. They are very much culturally conditioned with the consequent grave danger that they go out of date and leave us incomprehending.

C. The Abelardian Theory

Peter Abelard (1079-1142), in his commentary on the letter to the Romans, puts forward an exposition of the 'Moral Influence Theory' of atonement. It is an exemplarist view. The suffering of Christ is the supreme example of the cost of discipleship, and at the same time the cross is the completest possible demonstration of God's love (cf. Romans 8:32; Ch 5). While we were yet sinners Christ died for us. This great love, according to Abelard, may be expected to kindle a responding love in us and lead us into the true freedom of God's children. This whole approach requires a strong view of the incarnation. It lays great stress on the humanity of Jesus because his life and death as a whole are a response to divine love. God the Son's self-offering extends to the whole of his life as well as to death itself. It is a difficult view to expound rationally, although it is not unreasonable. Perhaps it simply has to be experienced. There is great emphasis on the graciousness of God and yet there is the real possibility, indeed appropriateness, of human response. The Abelardian view leaves space for active reception of God's love. It allows meaningful talk of a relationship between God and the human race. On the other hand it is sometimes objected that this theory really does not acknowledge the gravity of sin. However, the implicit idea of God experiencing suffering within the life of the Godhead is sufficient riposte. How much more grievously could the horror of human sin be felt?

This point is well brought out in Helen Waddell's *Life of Abelard*. She writes:

> Thibault was too happy for speech. He was busy unroping the little barrel, and Abelard had risen, the segment of cheese in his hand, to reach down their drinking-horns from the wall, when both men suddenly stood still.
>
> 'My God,' said Thibault, 'what's that?'
>
> From somewhere near them in the woods a cry had risen, a thin cry of such intolerable anguish that Abelard turned dizzy on his feet, and caught at the wall.
>
> 'It's a child's voice', he said. 'O God, are they at a child?'
>
> Thibault had gone outside. The cry came again, making the twilight and firelit hearth a mockery.
>
> 'A rabbit,' said Thibault. He listened. 'There's nothing worrying it. It'll be in a trap. Hugh told me he was putting them down. Christ!' The scream came again.
>
> Abelard was beside him, and the two plunged down the bank.

'Down by the river,' said Thibault. 'I saw them playing, God help them, when I was coming home. You know the way they go demented with fun in the evenings. It will have been drumming with its hind paws to itself and brought down the trap.'

Abelard went on, hardly listening. 'O God,' he was muttering. 'Let it die. Let it die quickly.'

But the cry came yet again. On the right, this time. He plunged through a thicket of hornbeam.

'Watch out,' said Thibault, thrusting past him. 'The trap might take the hand off you.'

The rabbit stopped shrieking when they stooped over it, either from exhaustion, or in some last extremity of fear. Thibault held the teeth of the trap apart, and Abelard gathered up the little creature in his hands. It lay for a moment breathing quickly, then in some blind recognition of the kindness that had met it at the last, the small head thrust and nestled against his arm, and it died.

It was that last confiding thrust that broke Abelard's heart. He looked down at the little draggled body, his mouth shaking. 'Thibault,' he said, 'do you think there is a God at all? Whatever has come to me, I earned it. But what did this one do?'

Thibault nodded.

'I know,' he said. 'Only – I think God is in it too.'

Abelard looked up sharply.

'In it? Do you mean that it makes him suffer, the way it does us?'

Again Thibault nodded.

'Then why doesn't he stop it?'

'I don't know,' said Thibault. 'Unless – unless it's like the Prodigal Son. I suppose the father could have kept him at home against his will. But what would have been the use? All this,' he

> stroked the limp body, 'is because of us. But all the time God suffers. More than we do.'[64]

The problem of subjective/objective atonement

One of the 'givens' of atonement theory is that it must be universal and objectively achieved apart from human activity. The basic plank in building any theory about what happened on the cross is the acknowledgement that human beings can do nothing about their own salvation. The offering of Christ was 'something accomplished, something done' once and for all. However, the subjective element consists in the fact that the atonement only becomes effective in the lives of human beings when they give themselves to God and to the achievement of his purpose. There are three movements in the experience of salvation.

(i) Initial justification

The imagery is of the law court where humanity stands in the dock condemned but receives a 'not guilty' verdict. God accepts the individual into a right relationship with himself. He forgives our unworthiness and our sin. God welcomes us as adoptive children. God's action is prior to everything else, but it can be seen from the human side as conversion, a coming to trust in God. It can be understood as a learning to love, a coming to repentance. It is centred on Christ, on union with him. God looks on us as we are in Christ and we come to him through Christ.

(ii) Sanctification

Initial justification is the first stage anticipating the final judgement. Sanctification is the process between the initial promise and the fulfilment of the promise at the last judgement. It is the process of becoming truly righteous which is yet not human achievement but God's work in us. Sanctification has an anchorage in the past and a forward orientation. It is due to God's grace and operates within the loving relationship between God and his creatures. It is our ongoing response to God. The keynote human response to God is thanksgiving. Gratitude is the prime Christian motive for action. Good works flow from it and are a sign of sanctification.

(iii) Final justification

The last judgement is basic to the apocalyptic expectation of the New Testament. We shall be judged according to our works (Matthew 16:27; 25:31-46; 2 Corinthians 5:10; James 2: 24; Revelation 20:12-13). Good works will not earn our salvation. God's justification of us is free and unmerited but we shall not be justified without works. Good works do not give us a right to justification but are a necessary condition of our final justification. There is no opposition between faith and works. Final justification is that point at which human beings have become irreversibly a part of God's creation as he finally intends it to be, the point at which our response is so God-directed that there is a moral irreversibility about it. This is nonetheless a free response and does not necessarily mean that growth ceases to take place.

Such a subject deserves much fuller description than the hasty and sketchy treatment it has received here. However, I hope that it is sufficient to give a flavour of the kind of reflection that has taken place concerning the objective fact that Jesus of Nazareth died a criminal's death on the hill of Calvary. Because the Church has never specified that one theory is to be preferred to another we are free to make our attempt to tell the story, but in telling the story we are bound to ask: What did God achieve in the Person of his Son by his death and resurrection? How are we to understand what happened on the cross? How does what happened affect the relationship between God and human beings? Any attempt to describe the reconciliation that was effected on the cross should be examined to ask whether it offers a worthy theology. What vision of God is offered? Is it consistent with what we have been taught to believe about God through Jesus Christ?

Some of the theories briefly described above fare better than others in this respect. Because so much that has been said by previous generations in the history of the

Church was necessarily socially conditioned we would do well to recognise that what we say is likely to have a sell-by date beyond which it will not speak to the times. We will not, however, readily dispense with what the tradition of the Church has said about atonement. The various descriptions of it should be kept like snapshots in the family album, side by side. Some will look exceedingly odd, but there will be moments when we will experience the cross as a victory of sorts, when we will feel that a load has been lifted from our shoulders, and when by looking at it we will be able to recognise the seriousness of God's claim to love us. In the Son God was prepared to go through suffering and death and there will be moments at least when we appreciate that somehow it was *for us*.

Ascension[65]

If death was not the end of the story, neither was the resurrection. It is all very well to proclaim that God has raised Jesus from the dead and that he has been seen by all sorts of people in many different places. How do we know that this was not merely a temporary phenomenon and that he did not die again? It is not enough to proclaim that he is alive. We must know that he is *still* alive. In fact, that is what Matthew asserts. At the beginning of his Gospel he tells the story of an angelic visitor to Joseph. He is not to be afraid to take Mary as his wife because the child she bears is *from the Holy Spirit* (1:20). Then Matthew says that this was in fulfilment of prophecy and he is to be called Emmanuel, 'God is with us' (1:23). Then at the end of the Gospel the very last words attributed to Jesus are:

> And remember, I am with you always, to the end of the age.

Jesus commissions his disciples and promises that he will *always* be with them.

The story of the ascension arises out a belief that Jesus is still alive. He did *not* die again. But then the story takes on a life of its own and illustrates other dimensions of Christian thinking about Jesus, things that must be true, given their foundational understanding that God had raised Jesus from the dead. They spoke of the ascension as:

1. The coronation of a king

Jesus had preached about the kingdom of God . . . what the world is like when God is in charge. By his elevation – the language of ascension is about 'going up' – the one who preached a message about the kingdom has become the king who rules over it. He takes his seat on his throne at the right hand of God. In our times kingdom language has for many people become suspect because it assumes a monarchical and hierarchical style of government. I do not know what is to be done about that. It certainly does not constitute an improvement to talk about God's republic! The important thing is to ask questions about the nature of the kingship which Jesus is said to exercise.

It is in terms of the book of Daniel (7:9-14) that the concept of absolute monarchy is modified. The kingdom of which the Bible speaks is a derivative form of rule, for the one to whom dominion and kingship is given is someone 'like a human being' who reigns at the behest of the Ancient of Days. His power comes from God, but this is the power of the one who washed his disciples' feet and who was identified with the pain and the suffering of the world through a criminal's death on the cross outside Jerusalem. This is the Servant King, the Shepherd King whose object is not to lord it over people like the rulers of this world but to do the will of God.

2. Going away to get closer

Presence is a funny thing. I can sit in the dentist's waiting room with a crowd of people and be closer to my wife who may be miles away than I am to anybody in that same room. That was certainly part of the experience of the first disciples. The more certain they were that Jesus Christ was with them, the more clearly they realised that they were not dependent upon being able to see him in the physical sense. They experienced the ascension as a going away, which, paradoxically, made him seem all the closer. The story of how he was taken away before their very eyes, with its back-flashes to the story of how Elijah was taken up to heaven in the presence of Elisha in a chariot of fire, gives the same assurance. 'As the LORD lives, and as you yourself live, I will not leave you.' (2 Kings 2:6).

3. Proper independence

> Do not hold on to me, because I have not yet ascended to the Father.
>
> John 20:17

There is a way of holding on which prevents the taking of free, responsible decisions. Jesus' words to Mary Magdalene point to the belief that it is God's will that those who serve him should do so of their own volition. There must be no unhealthy dependency, no clinging possessively. There must rather be space for a free relationship. Mary too has to be prepared to let Jesus go in order to feel his nearer presence.

4. The giving of the Spirit

At the same time the departure of Jesus is experienced as the access of new power. The disciples are not left floundering, wondering how they will cope. The ascension of Jesus makes way for the coming of the Holy Spirit (of which more below).

5. The giving of gifts

> When he ascended on high he made captivity
> itself a captive; he gave gifts to his people.
>
> Ephesians 4:8

The disciples believed that their divinely given task involved telling the story of Jesus and for this purpose they were sure that they had been given a power that they did not naturally possess. C P Snow in his powerful novel *The Corridors of Power* writes:

> The first thing is to get power; the second is to do something with it.

Christians have rather a sense of being given power which drives them out to preach in the service of their neighbour. It is not the power of compulsion which Jesus himself eschewed. It is the power of conviction, backed up by their own experience, which gave them strength for the task in hand.

6. Jesus took our humanity to heaven

The proclamation that Jesus ascended to the right hand of God is a doctrine of the Church replete with significance for us.

> He ascended into heaven
> and is seated at the right hand of God.

The body which he took to heaven is the earthly body still bearing the marks of crucifixion. His body was not prettified. He took suffering, scarred humanity in his own person to the very throne of God. The story indicates that there is no great unbridgeable gulf set between human beings and God. We are made for communion with him and belong in the presence of God. We are not so separated from God that we can have nothing to do with him. Jesus in another place is recorded as saying that he was going on ahead to prepare a place for us and the early Church believed that he was at the right hand of God to make intercession for us. With Jesus on our side there is nothing to fear. The many rich dimensions of the experience of the first disciples after the resurrection are translated for us into the story of the ascension. It contains profound teaching, insights which modern preachers must help the Church to recover.

Pentecost

> When the day of Pentecost had come, they were all together in one place. And suddenly from heaven there came a sound like the rush of a violent wind, and it filled the entire house where they were sitting. Divided tongues, as of fire, appeared among them, and a tongue rested on each of them. All of them were filled with the Holy Spirit and began to speak in other languages, as the Spirit gave them ability.
>
> Acts 2:1-4

There can be little doubt that in the up and down theology of Luke the ascension of Jesus to the right hand of the Father makes way for the coming of God's Holy Spirit. The giving of the ability to make themselves understood by people of many different languages is the evangelist's way of demonstrating the reversal of what happened at the Tower of Babel (Genesis 11:1-9) when human beings in their overweening pride reached up to heaven and their languages were scrambled. Whereas Babel is the symbol of disunity, Pentecost is the gift of the Spirit of unity, who creates community where formerly and in human terms there is none.

The Spirit, however, was in the continuing theological reflection of the first disciples a late developer! The debates about the relationship between the Spirit and the other Two Persons of the Trinity took place over a long period. There was consideration of whether or not divine titles could be attributed to the Spirit and as was the case with thinking about the Person of Christ, much of the reflection was overtaken by what early Christians felt able, even obliged, to say in worship.

It is, however, the Gospel of John which shows the most developed understanding of the work of the Spirit in the entire New Testament. He offers an alternative story about the giving of the Spirit, different from Luke's. After the resurrection Jesus appeared to his disciples. He identified himself by showing them his hands and his side. It is the same Jesus who was crucified who had come to them now to give them their commission.

> Peace be with you. As the Father has sent me, so I send you.' When he had said this, he breathed on them, and said to them, 'Receive the Holy Spirit . . .'
>
> John 20:21-22

It might be claimed that in the teaching of John the Holy Spirit is Christ's other self, for it is through the Spirit that the presence of Christ is universalised. The Spirit, after the physical departure of Jesus Christ, makes possible his indwelling. There is a very close connection between Jesus and the Spirit.[66]

The functions of the Holy Spirit in the New Testament are numerous. It is through the Spirit that the believer confesses that 'Jesus is Lord' (1 Corinthians 12:3). The Spirit is the source of holiness in Christian believers. They are saints because they have received the Holy Spirit into their lives. The Spirit inspires prayer. It is by the Spirit that we cry 'Abba, Father' (Romans 8:15). The presence of the Spirit is the promise and anticipation of our place within God's kingdom. The Spirit is a down-payment on what is to come. The Spirit, as I have already indicated, is the source of Christian unity within the one body but it is a differentiated unity. We are each given different gifts but because they are gifts of the Spirit, they are ordered for the common good and for the flourishing of the community. There is not space to give an extended account of each of these spheres of activity of the Spirit, but there is one Johannine statement which demands further elaboration.

> . . . the Advocate, the Holy Spirit, whom the Father will send in my name, will teach you everything, and remind you of all that I have said to you.
>
> John 14:26

Many people are very good at being wise after the event. They are completely and utterly useless in a crisis. They have nothing to say in the face of a current problem but once events have taken their course and the situation has been resolved with everybody's behaviour identified and labelled, they stand there solemnly saying: 'Well, you know, I could have told you that's what he'd do. I knew she'd say that. Of course, if you know them like I know them, you might have known too.' They are full of wisdom but they are only wise after the event. In fact, I know more people with PhDs in Hindsight than in any other subject.

The disciples of Jesus all had PhDs in Hindsight. And there is a real sense in which it could hardly have been otherwise. They had listened a great deal to what Jesus had to say. They saw what he did. But they either plainly did not understand what he was up to, or they only partially understood. Much that he said and did was just not grasped until after his death and he had been raised to life again. It was only in the light of the resurrection that the greater part of the life and activity of Jesus made any sense at all, even to those disciples who were closest to him. 'Do you remember when he said that the Father would send the Holy Spirit? He said the Spirit would teach us everything and would call to mind everything he'd told us.' And they started to remember this and remember that . . . and things that had seemed so mysterious at the time suddenly made sense.

There were many things during Jesus' lifetime which they had not understood or not been prepared to swallow. One major sticking point had been when Jesus had begun to make it plain that the Messiah would have to suffer and to die. At Caesarea Philippi Jesus asked his disciples who people thought he was. Well, some say you are John the Baptist come back to life; some say you are Elijah or one of the other prophets. Yes, but who do you think I am? Then Peter has that tremendous flash of insight. You are the Christ, the Messiah, the promised king. The trouble is Jesus went on to tell them how the Messiah must suffer and die. They could not get their minds round that. It was not possible. The promised king could not suffer.

In fact, the disciples only got their heads around this painful recognition after it had happened. He had gone through a mockery of a trial. They had abandoned him and betrayed him and denied him. He had been whipped and abused and crucified, and suddenly they remembered Caesarea Philippi and how he had said that that's the way it had to be. They ought not to have been surprised but they were only prepared to accept it after it had happened and the Holy Spirit had come to teach them what they needed to know and to remind them of what Jesus had said.

What is said in John 14:26 seems to fit my experience. The guidance of the Holy Spirit and the teaching we receive through the Holy Spirit is very largely an over-the-shoulder, hindsight operation. It often acts as a confirmation of the rightness of what has happened rather than as a finger beckoning from the future. The Spirit calls to mind those things which are already stored there, acting as a trigger to memory. Things are brought to the front of the mind and connections are made which were not previously tied up. We are given insight into the rightness of what happened in the past and into the consequences of the choices we made for the present and the future. When I worked on building sites in university vacations it did not seem at the time to have any greater importance than earning cash to keep body and soul together. When a few years later one part of my work as headmaster of the Methodist Secondary School in Dabou meant physically building staff housing and classrooms, I was very glad someone had taught me how to mix concrete and to put up shuttering! Pure coincidence? In West Africa it certainly felt like preparation for my job there.

Of course we can be guided by the Spirit through prayer and the study of the Scriptures. However, we can be sure that any guidance concerning the way forward will not be disconnected from the past. It will be consonant with the whole. It will make sense both backwards and forwards. Reflection on the meaning of the Scriptures for us and communion with God are things which take place in the context of the lives we have lived to this point. The Holy Spirit helps us to reflect on the experience we have already had and through prayer and Bible study helps us make sense of what has gone before so that we may better understand the way ahead.

Two words of warning about the way the Spirit leads us.

1. Feeling guided does not necessarily mean that we are right.

(a) Our individual sense of direction has to be tested against the perceptions of the Church, which is why when people feel called to ministry the Church examines that sense of call to try and determine whether or not it is genuine.

(b) 'The Lord has told me to tell you this.' It is my experience that when someone comes to me saying that they have a message for me from the Lord, usually they are being highly manipulative. The Spirit should not be used as a blunt instrument to compel me to do what the speaker wants. Unless the Lord has told me too . . .

2. Guidance does not have to be conveyed in a spectacular manner. Few get the blinding light on the Damascus road. One major vehicle used by the Holy Spirit is our basic (God-given) common sense. There are many things for which we do not need to seek guidance because God has already equipped us with the means of making many decisions unaided, through our native wit. This gift is not

to be despised. We must use our common sense. None the less it remains true that

> the advocate, the Holy Spirit whom the Father will send in my name, will teach you everything and remind you of all that I have told you.

We have to immerse ourselves in that teaching and learn to trust the guidance which comes through our ordinary everyday experience. We will find that true guidance is coherent with all that has gone before. If it is a fruit of the Spirit it will be anchored in our relationship with Jesus Christ and bring glory to the Father.

Trinity

The Jews, the Muslims, the Christians all claim to be monotheists. They say that God is One. Yet it cannot be said that they share the same understanding of the Unity of the Godhead for Christians have what has been called 'a differentiated Oneness'. God is One God in Three Persons. In relation to God three is a strange number, as Robert Pirsig has pointed out.

> The metaphysician normally seeks either a monism, such as God, which explains the nature of the world as a manifestation of one single thing, or he seeks a dualism, such as mind-matter, which explains it as two things, or he leaves it as a pluralism, which explains it as a manifestation of an indefinite number of things. But three is an awkward number.[67]

The doctrine of the Trinity is for many people a theological conundrum. How can one + one + one equal one? I remember my children years ago showing me how working with a different base it is possible mathematically, but the Trinity is not a way of conjuring with figures. It is an attempt to explain what the first disciples experienced. They were Jews who knew that there is One God. This God they came to know through Jesus as the Father. They believed that Jesus was the Son of God and with his ascension, his return to the Father, they received an influx of power which they described as the Spirit of God. They experienced God in his three ways of being God. However, the starting-point of their awareness of God's three-in-oneness was in the life of Jesus. So for us, our way into the doctrine has to be christological. It is indeed our judgement about who or what Jesus was which affects our understanding of the Godhead. For me the doctrine of the Trinity has never been an abstraction which could safely be left on one side.

I was born and brought up in a Unitarian family. I went to church and Sunday school three times every Sunday until one day my mother and father had a stand-up row with the minister, going off in the traditional huff vowing never again to darken the doors of his church. Suddenly I had nowhere to go . . . until a school friend asked me to go with him to the youth club. It turned out to be a Methodist youth club. We played billiards, snooker and table tennis. It was a very short step from the youth club to the young people's group which met every Sunday. Both were run by the same people. I got caught up in the life of that church and experienced through the fellowship of the congregation and through the preaching ministry of the local Methodist minister what I believed to be the presence of the risen Christ. I had always been taught that Jesus of Nazareth was a man to be honoured. He was a great Jewish prophet, but there was no way in which he was son of God in any way different from anybody else. I came to believe that he was more than that, in fact that he was Son of God and Messiah, that he was the Second Person of the Trinity. When my parents did return to the Unitarian Church they set the minister on me to straighten me out. He got nowhere in spite of the wonderful logic of his arguments. It is very difficult to argue with someone with an experience! Certainly the mainstream Church's teaching about the Trinity has always been important to me.

Nevertheless, like many people, for a long time whilst my faith grew and developed I was effectively binitarian rather than trinitarian. For me it was the understanding of God as Spirit which did not get much of a look-in. That was the point at which my understanding of God lacked the fullness it was later to acquire. I suspect that many Christians operate with less than a full-blown trinitarian understanding of the being of God. It must be a part of the task of the preacher to help people achieve the fullness of the Christian vision. In Christian terms Jesus Christ is truly and fully God but he is not the whole of God. The doctrine of the Trinity is an attempt to say that there is more to God than Father; there is more to God than Son; there is more to God than Spirit. We need some grasp of God's three-in-oneness to attain to the full Christian vision of the relationships within the Godhead.

It is possible to begin a study of the Trinity from the assertion that God is One-in-Three. It is equally possible to begin with the statement that God is Three-in-One. In the Western Church the former has been the dominating tendency, with the result sometimes when this approach was overstressed, that it wandered into unitarianism. In the Eastern Church with the latter starting-point it was easy at times to talk as if there are three gods. The debates of the Early Church were concerned to avoid these two outcomes and the result was some very complicated theological clarification of the relationships amongst Father, Son and Holy Spirit, which most people today do not find particularly illuminating. Beginning with the Oneness end of the equation our spiritual forbears spoke of the 'coinherence' of the Three Persons of the Trinity. The Three Persons mutually interpenetrate, interpermeate, contain and fill each other, so that the operations of the Trinity towards the world are undivided. At the same time, starting from the Threeness they affirmed that certain activities of the Trinity vis-à-vis the world are appropriately attributed to one or other of the persons of the Trinity. There can be no doubt that orthodoxy required this kind of definition and precision in speaking of God as Trinity in order to rule what it was permissible and not permissible to say. Many people today nevertheless find this kind of debate pretty sterile and wonder if such a struggle to understand is worth it. For those who are called upon to expound the Church's doctrine the debate must continue in order to seek better and clearer ways of expounding the truths which our Christian ancestors were trying to protect and in order to demonstrate what the doctrine of the Trinity might mean in practical terms.

Also if the doctrine of the Trinity is truly a description of what God is like then every theological statement will have a trinitarian dimension. Many modern writers have worked this through in relation to specific pieces of teaching. For example, for a trinitarian understanding of atonement the reader should consult Jürgen Moltmann's seminal work *The Crucified God*[68]; for an understanding of Church and the Church's mission in terms of the Trinity, see the writings of Lesslie Newbigin, *The Household of God*[69] and *The Open Secret*[70]. The instances can be multiplied. For example, the beginning of St John's Gospel offers an alternative account of the beginning of things. He does not make use of a Virgin birth story. He talks about the Word, the Logos, a concept which has roots in Greek philosophy and in the Wisdom literature of the Old Testament. John's reflection on the significance of Jesus Christ leads him to think about the pre-existence of Christ. If this Jesus Christ was indeed God in action in his world there was never a time when he did not exist.

> In the beginning was the Word, and the Word was with God, and the Word was God. All things came into being through him, and without him not one thing came into being. What has come into being in him was life, and the life was the light of all people. The light shines in the darkness and the darkness did not overcome it.
>
> John 1:1-5

John presents us with a differentiated Unity – the Word was *with* God – yet a Unity none the less. The Word was *God*. However, not only was Jesus Christ there in the beginning. His activity in creation with all the echoes of the beginning of the book of Genesis is spelled out. The doctrine of creation, which in Genesis involves God and the spirit of God, becomes fully trinitarian as the role of the pre-existent Christ is reflected back from a consideration of who this Jesus Christ must really be. John is following through the logic of the act of obeisance which is found at the end of his Gospel when Thomas worships at the feet of Jesus with the words: 'My Lord and my God!'

In recent times, however, the way in which the usefulness of the doctrine of the Trinity has most been illustrated is in terms of the inner life of the Godhead, Father, Son and Holy Spirit, as the pattern of all community. Our vision of God has at its heart a community of the co-equal, co-eternal Three. Here there is no hierarchy, no dominance of one by either of the others. Here is a vision of harmony, which is described by the beautiful notion of 'perichoresis', an everlasting dancing around together, three partners acting in unison. It is again Jürgen Moltmann in his earth-breaking book on *The Trinity and the Kingdom of God*[71] who spells out the implications of such teaching for the structure and practice of human community, both inside and outside the Church. Our thinking and our ways of acting together would be revolutionised if we took the doctrine of the Trinity, God's way of being God, as the pattern of our life together.

EPILOGUE

Speaking of dissatisfaction with what is called doctrinal preaching, Phillips Brooks was emphatic:

> The truth is, no preaching ever had any strong power that was not the preaching of doctrine. The preachers that have moved and held men [sic] have always preached doctrine. No exhortation to a good life that does not put behind it some truth as deep as eternity can seize and hold the conscience. Preach doctrine, preach all the doctrine that you know, and learn forever more and more; but preach it always, not that men [sic] may believe it, but that men may be saved by believing it. So it shall be live, not dead.[72]

I have claimed that the primary method of communication preachers should use is story. The teaching which was extrapolated from the story of the life, death and resurrection of Jesus must become story in order that our hearers may receive in their own experience the truth that we intend to communicate.

It is said that the road to hell is paved with good intentions. It might be replied that the road to heaven is paved with good intentions, for we should not have less than 'good' intentions. In our preparation of ourselves and of what we have to say we will be eternal students. We will 'learn forever more and more'. With the intention of being better preachers of the gospel, we will do all we can to enlarge our own experience in order that we and our hearers may be enriched. The story we tell should never be reduced to a message, for the story ought to have its own integrity. It should be possible for our hearers to step inside it and experience it for themselves. In such a way it will never be reduced to a moral tale.

Let me finally return to the intention with which we step into the pulpit. It must not be to make a display of ourselves but to focus on Jesus Christ so that the preaching becomes an event in which we may hope that the hearer will encounter God. We should be offering the best we can. Our preparation should be as full and rigorous as possible. We should have a clear vision of what it is that we are trying to get across but what we do will always be less than the best. Even though it may be the best of which we are capable, when all is said and done, our offering will be imperfect. All we have to do is give it over to God and ask him to use it. If our intention is right God will accept it and use it for his purposes. It is only God who can make our words his word. However, the evidence of the centuries is that he has used frail human beings to lead others into his presence. Acknowledging our frailty and our inadequacy should not be an excuse for giving up on our preparation, though we may be allowed to recognise it for our comfort and encouragement. God can make use even of us. We can go on praying that he will allow us 'to be a window, through his grace'.

SELECT BIBLIOGRAPHY ON PREACHING

Karl Barth, *Prayer and Preaching*, SCM Press Limited, London 1964.

Phillips Brooks, *Lectures on Preaching*, Allenson, London 1902.

David Buttrick, *A Captive Voice: The Liberation of Preaching*, Westminster John Knox Press, Louisville, Kentucky 1994.

David Buttrick, *Preaching the NEW and the NOW*, Westminster John Knox Press, Louisville, Kentucky 1998.

Donald English, *An Evangelical Theology of Preaching*, Abingdon Press, Nashville 1996.

Thomas G Long and Edward Farley, [Editors], *Preaching as a Theological Task: World, Gospel, Scripture, In honor of David Buttrick*, Westminster John Knox Press, Louisville, Kentucky 1996.

Johnston R McKay, *This Small Pool*, The Mair Lectures, University of Glasgow 1995, Trinity St Mungo Press, Glasgow 1997.

Colin Morris, *Raising the Dead: The Art of the Preacher as Public Performer*, Fount 1996.

Gail R O'Day & Thomas G Long, [Editors], *Listening to the Word: Studies in honor of Fred B Craddock*, Abingdon Press, Nashville 1993.

William E Sangster, *The Craft of Sermon Construction*, Pickering & Inglis, London & Glasgow 1954.

Michael J Townsend, *Story*, Methodist Publishing House, 1991.

J Philip Wogaman, *Speaking the Truth in Love: Prophetic Preaching to a Broken World*, Westminster John Knox Press, Louisville, Kentucky 1998.

NOTES

Foreword

1. 'The Windows' by George Herbert in *Poet to Poet, George Herbert* selected by W H Auden, Penguin Books 1973, p.61.

2. *Lectures on Preaching* delivered by the Rt Revd Phillips Brooks before the Divinity School of Yale College 1877, published Allenson, London 1902.

Chapter 1

3. cf. John Macquarrie, *Principles of Christian Theology,* SCM Press, London 1966: 'Theology may be defined as the study which, through participation in and reflection upon a religious faith, seeks to express the content of this faith in the clearest and most coherent language available' p.1.

4. Published as *This Small Pool,* Studies in Practical Theology No 2, Trinity St Mungo Press 1997.

5. Fred B Craddock, 'The Gospel of God' in Thomas Long and Edward Farley (Editors) *Preaching as a Theological Task: World, Gospel, Scripture In Honor of David Buttrick,* Westminster John Knox Press, Louisville, Kentucky 1996 p.80.

6. David M Greenhaw, 'The Formation of Consciousness' in Thomas Long and Edward Farley (Editors) *Preaching as a Theological Task: World, Gospel, Scripture, In Honor of David Buttrick,* Westminster John Knox Press, Louisville, Kentucky 1996 p.8.

7. *The Doctrine Commission of the Church of England, Christian Believing*, SPCK, London, 1976, p.31.

8. Leonard Hodgson, *For Faith and Freedom*, Part III, Lecture I on the Bible, The Gifford Lectures, 1955-57, in the University of Glasgow, SCM Press, London 1968.

9. J L Houlden, Exploration in Theology Vol. 3 p.23.

10. See Blaise Pascal's statement about the Wager cf. Pensées 418 and the discussion of it in Hans Küng's *Does God Exist?* Collins, London, 1980.

11. David Buttrick, *A Captive Voice: The Liberation of Preaching*, Westminster John Knox Press, Louisville, Kentucky, 1994, pp.16-17.

12. Gail O'Day in Gail O'Day & Thomas Long (Editors) *Listening to the Word: Studies in honor of Fred B Craddock*, Abingdon Press, Nashville, 1993, p.32.

13. William K Carl III – 'Twin Covenants in Tension on the Eve of the Twenty-first Century' in Thomas Long and Edward Farley (Editors) *Preaching as a Theological Task: World, Gospel, Scripture, In Honor of David Buttrick*, Westminster John Knox Press, Louisville, Kentucky 1996 p.54.

14. *The Doctrine Commission of the Church of England Christian Believing*, SPCK, London 1976, p.41.

15. *The Doctrine Commission of the Church of England Christian Believing*, SPCK, London 1976, p.33.

16. Thomas M Morrow, Raymond J Billington and James B Bates *Worship and Preaching* Revised Edition, The Epworth Press 1967, p.101.

Chapter 2

17. Hosea 1:8

18. Quoted by Johnston R McKay, *This Small Pool*, from Richard Holloway, *The Folly of Preaching in Paradoxes of Christian Faith and Life.*

19. Christine Pilkington, *Preaching on the Old Testament* The Preacher's Library Vol 2, Foundery Press, Peterborough, p.19.

20. Thomas G Long, 'Learning to speak about sin' in Thomas Long and Edward Farley (Editors) *Preaching as a Theological Task: World, Gospel, Scripture, In Honor of David Buttrick*, Westminster John Knox Press, Louisville, Kentucky 1996 p.102.

21. Donald English, *An Evangelical Theology of Preaching*, Abingdon Press, 1996, p.83.

22. Donald English, *An Evangelical Theology of Preaching*, Abingdon Press, 1996, p.122.

23. Amos 1:3-5.

24. Mark 4:11-12.

25. Mark 4:33-34.

26. F F Bruce, *The Hard Sayings of Jesus*, Hodder & Stoughton, London 1983 p.100.

27. Johnston R McKay, *This Small Pool: The Mair Lectures – University of Glasgow, 1995*, Trinity St Mungo Press, 1997, p.52.

28. Johnston R McKay, *This Small Pool: The Mair Lectures – University of Glasgow, 1995*, Trinity St Mungo Press, 1997, p.53.

29. Gene M Tucker, 'Reading and Preaching the Old Testament' in Gail O'Day & Thomas G Long (Editors), *Listening to the Word: Studies in Honor of Fred B Craddock*, Abingdon Press, Nashville 1993 p.39.

30. David Buttrick, *A Captive Voice: The Liberation of Preaching*, Westminster John Knox Press, Louisville, Kentucky, 1994, p.67

31. Gerd Theissen, *The Shadow of the Galilean*, SCM Press Ltd, 1987, p.115-116.

Chapter 3

32. Matthew 4:19

33. Albert Schweitzer, *The Quest of the Historical Jesus*, 3rd Eng Edition, 1956, A & C Black, London, p.401.

34. Matthew 3:17.

35. Matthew 4:3.

36. Matthew 3:2 in the mouth of John; Matthew 4:17 on the lips of Jesus.

37. Luke 6:20-26.

38. Genesis 12:7.

39. Matthew 1:23.

40. Luke 4:18-19.

41. Luke 1:51-53.

42. See Matthew 19:16-26.

43. See Matthew 16:13-20.

44. Matthew 16:16.

45. Matthew 16:21-22.

46. Mark 9:2-13; Luke 9:28-36; 2 Peter 1:16-18.

47. Matthew 17:5.

48. Ibid.

49. 2 Peter 1:16-18.

50. Matthew 17:9.

51. Daniel 7:13-14. The NRSV footnote has 'one like a son of man'.

52. Matthew 18:3-5.

53. Matthew 20:20-23.

54. Matthew 20: 25-28.

55. John 13:1-20.

56. John 18:11.

57. Matthew 26:36-46.

58. Endo, *Silence,* Peter Owen 1976, p.271.

59. Mark 15:39 & footnote.

60. Matthew 28:19.

61. John 20:28.

Chapter 4

62. One part of the synoptic tradition sees the recognition of Jesus as Messiah in the story of the transfiguration where Jesus is seen in the presence of Elijah, the archetypal prophet, and Moses, the supreme

Lawgiver. In such a way he is declared to be the fulfilment of both the Law and the Prophets.

63. E Brooks Holifield in *Theology Today* 'On saying too little and saying too much'.

64 Helen Waddell, *Peter Abelard,* Collins, Fontana Books, 1958, p.240-241.

65. Matthew 28:16-20; Mark 16:19-20 (in the longer ending); Luke 24:44-53; Acts 1:6-11; Ephesians 1:15-23.

66. But not uniquely in John. See also in Paul, Romans 8:9; Philippians 1:19 'the Spirit of Jesus Christ' and Galatians 4:6 'the Spirit of his Son'.

67. Robert M Pirsig, *Zen and the Art of Motor Cycle Maintenance,* Corgi Books, London 1979, p.233. Pirsig himself offers a kind of trinity of mind, matter and quality, where quality is his governing principle.

68. Jürgen Moltmann, *The Crucified God*, SCM Press, London, 1974.

69. Lesslie Newbigin, *The Household of God*, SCM Press, London , 1953.

70. Lesslie Newbigin, *The Open Secret*, SPCK, London, 1978.

71. Jürgen Moltmann, *The Trinity and the Kingdom of God*, SCM Press, London, 1981.

Epilogue

72. *Lectures on Preaching* delivered by the Rt Revd Phillips Brooks before the Divinity School of Yale College 1877, published Allenson, London, 1902.